CHOOSING THE
PRESIDENT
2008

4/08

CHOOSING THE PRESIDENT 2008

A Citizen's Guide to the Electoral Process

LEAGUE OF WOMEN VOTERS®

Edited by Bob Guldin

THE LYONS PRESS
Guilford, Connecticut
An Imprint of The Globe Pequot Press

To buy books in quantity for corporate use
or incentives, call **(800) 962–0973**
or e-mail **premiums@GlobePequot.com.**

The Lyons Press is an imprint of The Globe Pequot Press.

Designed by John Barnett/4 Eyes Design

Library of Congress Cataloging-in-Publication Data is available on file.

ISBN 978-1-59921-214-2

Printed in the United States of America

10 9 8 7 6 5 4 3 2 1

CONTENTS

FOREWORD

Choosing the President 2008, published by the League of Women Voters Education Fund, is an important publication with a rich history. It is part of a proud League tradition of providing a step-by-step guide to the process by which we elect our presidents. Previous editions cover more than eleven presidential election cycles.

This latest edition reflects important and ongoing changes in the way the presidential election is experienced by voters in the twenty-first century. In the 2004 edition, we introduced two then-very-new laws—the Help America Vote Act of 2002 (HAVA) and the Bipartisan Campaign Reform Act of 2002 (BCRA). In this 2008 edition, we incorporate the impact of these two major pieces of reform legislation, which were tested and reflected in the 2004 presidential and 2006 federal elections. We do note, however, that the U.S. Supreme Court in 2007 seriously reduced in scope an important section of BCRA, so that the law will not have as big an impact on the 2008 presidential election as previously expected.

While the constitutional process of choosing the president remains much as it has been for more than two hundred years, the context in which it takes place would be unrecognizable to voters of earlier generations. The presidential election process is constantly evolving. The importance of electronic media and the Internet, the enormous and ever growing role of money in politics, the crisis in public funding of presidential campaigns, and the increased front-loading of the primary election schedule are just some of the factors that influence the way the presidential campaign unfolds today.

The organization of this book into two parts, "The Players" and "The Process," is designed to help readers put all of the complex pieces together in an easy-to-understand way.

Choosing the President 2008 was edited by Bob Guldin, the Washington, D.C.-area writer and editor who also edited the 2004 edition.

The League gratefully acknowledges the preparers of earlier editions, particularly William H. Woodwell, who wrote the 2000 edition, whose work, in turn, owed a great deal to the League's 1984 edition, as well as the 1992 edition published by the League of Women Voters of California Education Fund. We appreciate the expertise provided to this edition's editor by Thomas Patterson, Bradlee Professor of Politics and the Press, Kennedy School of Government, Harvard University. We also thank LWVUS staff members Nancy Tate, Lloyd Leonard, Jeanette Senecal, and Shirley Tabata Ponomareff for their contributions to this 2008 edition.

Finally, we wish to express our appreciation to League members and other volunteers across the country who provide accessible information and services to voters, and especially to all Americans who participate in choosing the president.

MARY G. WILSON
President, League of Women Voters of the United States
June 2007

INTRODUCTION

The U.S. presidential election is the biggest event in American politics. It's an exciting and complicated process that begins immediately after the preceding election and doesn't end until you, the voter, have your say. (And as we learned in the amazing aftermath of the 2000 presidential election, it's possible for the campaign to continue even after Election Day.)

What happens during this extended campaign is a quest not just for votes, but also for political contributions, favorable media coverage, Internet attention, endorsements, and all the other makings of a winning candidacy for the highest elected office in America. Key events along the way include the primaries and caucuses, the party conventions, and the debates—not to mention all the speeches, polls, and focus groups, plus the barrage of radio and television commercials imploring you to vote this way or that.

It's easy to be overwhelmed. And that's why the League of Women Voters produced this book. Trying to follow the presidential election without an understanding of what's going on and why is like watching a foreign-language film without the subtitles. You may get a general idea about the plot and characters, but you'll miss out on what's really happening. You'll miss a lot of the drama as well.

The presidential election process is constantly evolving. The advent of television and then the Internet, the increasing role of money in politics, an ever-accelerating schedule of primary elections, and ups and downs in voter interest are just a few of the developments that have transformed the way we choose the president.

Among the latest changes covered in *Choosing the President 2008* are:

- The growing diversity among those running for president, with a woman, an African-American, and a Mormon among the top tier of candidates, as of 2007
- Transformations in the mass media, as Internet sites such as YouTube and MySpace gain real influence and newspapers and network news decline in importance
- The shift of most primary elections to February 2008, which may give the United States something resembling a national primary for the first time ever
- The crisis in public funding of presidential candidates.

In the pages that follow, you'll learn more about these and many other issues. This book doesn't tell you how to vote. But it does try to explain why certain things happen the way they do—for example, why the campaigning starts so early, why money is so important, and why some states are deluged with campaign ads, while others are almost entirely ignored.

Choosing the President also offers pointers for getting the most out of the election by directing you to the best political Web sites, helping you evaluate news coverage, and suggesting what to look for when you watch the debates and the conventions or try to make sense of all the polls and television and radio ads. This book can be read from cover to cover or picked up as needed when you want to know more about what's happening, or about something in the news.

A presidential election is your opportunity to shape this country's future and have a say in important issues that affect your life. With a clearer understanding of what's involved in choosing the president, you'll be better equipped to follow the campaign and better able to make an informed decision come Election Day.

—*League of Women Voters*

PART I

THE PLAYERS

CHAPTER 1

We the People

The most important players in the election of a U.S. president are not the candidates or their staffs, not the political parties or the other organizations with a stake in the outcome, and not the media pundits who often try to tell us what we think. No, as hard as it is to remember sometimes, a presidential election revolves around the beliefs and the actions of American voters. Come Election Day, no one else's opinions matter, and no one else has control over the outcome.

Voting is the great equalizer in American society. No matter how much money you have or who your friends are or whether or not you contributed to a particular candidate, you have one vote—the same as everybody else. And with that one vote, you have the power to influence decisions that will affect your life. Your job, your taxes, your health care, your Social Security, whether the nation goes to war, you name it—they are all at stake.

It's Been a Long Road: Voting in the Nation's Early Years

Today, every American citizen age eighteen and older has the right to vote. Sometimes it's a right we take for granted. We forget how much hard work and how much blood, sweat, and tears have gone into expanding the franchise, or making sure that all segments of the American population—minorities, women, youth, and others—are able to have their say.

Despite their opposition to arbitrary rule and their faith in popular sovereignty, the founders of the United States did not believe that all adults should be able to vote. During the early years of the country's history, legislatures in the United States generally restricted voting to white males who were twenty-one or older. Many states also limited voting rights to those who "had a stake in society." Translation: To vote, you had to own property. State governments began to eliminate the property requirement during the 1820s and 1830s.

By the time of the Civil War, almost all states had broadened the right to vote to all adult free males, property owners or not; black males had won the right to vote in most Northern states. In the decades since, the power base of American democracy has gradually widened, moving the nation closer and closer to the vision set forth in the Declaration of Independence of a government that derives its power from "the consent of the governed."

Opening Democracy's Door: Expanding the Franchise

The U.S. Constitution left it to the states to determine precisely who was qualified to vote. As a result, expanding voting rights to Americans who had been turned away or discouraged from voting has required either: (1) a constitutional amendment to make it the law of the land that certain groups cannot be denied the right to vote; or (2) changes in federal law to remove barriers to registration and voting and to make it easier for all Americans to have their say. To this day, the states still set the basic qualifications for voting, but they may not turn away certain categories of people, thanks to a series of constitutional amendments:

- The Fifteenth Amendment, ratified in 1870, ensured that Americans could not be denied the right to vote on account of their race. The amendment was one of three that were ratified in the Reconstruction era following the Civil War in an effort to guarantee equal rights for African-Americans. The other Reconstruction amendments were the Thirteenth, which outlawed slavery, and the Fourteenth, which guaranteed equal protection under the law for all citizens, regardless of their race.

+ The Nineteenth Amendment, ratified in 1920, marked the end of a decades-long struggle for equal voting rights for women. By 1916, women were able to vote in only twelve states; the vast majority of American women were still denied this fundamental right. In the end, the fight for women's voting rights was led by the National American Woman Suffrage Association, the precursor of today's League of Women Voters.

+ The Twenty-sixth Amendment is the most recent constitutional amendment relating to the right to vote. Ratified in 1971, it extended the vote to anyone eighteen years of age and over. Until then, states had generally restricted voting to the twenty-one-and-over population.

+ Other constitutional amendments have expanded the electorate in different ways—with the Twenty-third (ratified in 1961) allowing residents of the District of Columbia to vote for president, and the Twenty-fourth (1964) outlawing the poll taxes that discouraged poor people, mostly African-Americans, from voting in many Southern states. It is hard to believe today, but poll taxes meant that people actually had to pay to vote.

KNOWING YOUR RIGHTS

FIFTEENTH AMENDMENT, Section 1. The right of citizens of the United States to vote shall not be denied or abridged by the United States or by any State on account of race, color, or previous condition of servitude. (Ratified in 1870)

NINETEENTH AMENDMENT, Section 1. The right of citizens of the United States to vote shall not be denied or abridged by the United States or by any State on account of sex. (Ratified in 1920)

TWENTY-FOURTH AMENDMENT, Section 1. The right of citizens of the United States to vote in any primary or other election for President or Vice President, for electors for President or Vice President, or for Senator or Representative in Congress, shall not be denied or abridged by the United States or any State by reason of failure to pay any poll tax or other tax. (Ratified in 1964)

TWENTY-SIXTH AMENDMENT, Section 1. The right of citizens of the United States, who are eighteen years of age or older, to vote shall not be denied or abridged by the United States or by any State on account of age. (Ratified in 1971)

Together, these constitutional changes have had the effect of legally extending the eligibility to vote to all U.S. citizens over eighteen years of age, with the exception in most states of convicted felons.

Unfinished Business: Lowering the Barriers to Voting

The fact that the Constitution told states they couldn't deny certain groups the right to vote didn't keep states from erecting barriers to registration and voting—barriers ensuring that certain groups would be underrepresented at the polls.

In the late nineteenth century, in fact, many Southern states tried to get around the Fifteenth Amendment's guarantee of equal voting rights for blacks by adding "grandfather clauses" to their state constitutions. These clauses generally limited the right to vote to those individuals who had been able to vote before the Fifteenth Amendment became law, along with their descendants. The Supreme Court declared these laws unconstitutional in the early twentieth century.

Poll taxes were an early example of the other barriers facing African-Americans and other minorities seeking to exercise their right to vote. Over the years, states also have used literacy tests and English-language requirements, length-of-residency requirements, and onerous voter-registration rules to keep registration and voting rates down among racial and ethnic minorities, the poor, and other groups, such as college students.

In recent decades, two major pieces of federal legislation have sought to break down these and other barriers to registration and voting: the Voting Rights Act, originally enacted in 1965; and the National Voter Registration Act, signed into law in 1993.

The Voting Rights Act

The Voting Rights Act is a complex and detailed law, but its basic goal is to make sure that racial minorities, no matter where they live, have the same opportunity as other citizens to participate in the nation's political life. The law was enacted to try to stop some of the common practices that restricted African-American voting in many Southern states.

Passage of the Voting Rights Act happened shortly after civil rights activists organized a protest march in Selma, Alabama, in March 1965, with the goal of drawing national attention to the struggle for black voting rights. Violence erupted as police brutally attacked the marchers on a day that came to be known as Bloody Sunday. Another march was organized two weeks later and culminated in an address by the Reverend Martin Luther King, Jr., that drew twenty thousand people to the state capital of Montgomery. The episode created new support for the Voting Rights Act, which President Lyndon Johnson signed into law that August.

The following are some of the law's key provisions:

- No citizen can be prevented from voting in presidential elections because of length-of-residency requirements.
- No one can deny an eligible citizen the right to vote or interfere with or intimidate anyone seeking to register to vote.
- Literacy tests and other methods cannot be used as qualifications for voting in any federal, state, local, general, or primary election.
- Seven states and a number of local jurisdictions with a historical pattern of discrimination based on race must submit any changes in their election laws to the U.S. Justice Department for approval.

In 1975, Congress added provisions to the act to make sure that U.S. citizens are not deprived of the right to vote because they cannot read, write, or speak English. Another series of amendments in 1982 provided that Americans with disabilities cannot be prohibited from bringing someone else to the polls to help them vote, so long as that person is not the voter's employer or union representative. In 2006, Congress passed a twenty-five-year extension of the Voting Rights Act with all its provisions.

But even with the Voting Rights Act and its additional protections on the books, minorities and other groups continued to face difficulties in registration and voting. Intimidation, misleading information, and poor service to minority registrants still were widely reported in the 2004 election. Sometimes discrimination can take subtle forms. For example, in the hotly contested 2000 presidential election, black voters in Florida were more likely than whites to have their votes ruled invalid. One reason for this may have been that predominantly African-American precincts were more likely to have old voting machines and poorly trained poll workers.

In many states, the law for many years required citizens to appear in person during weekday hours to register to vote, overlooking the fact that large numbers of residents—many of them lower-income, hourly workers—couldn't get away from their jobs. In addition, some elections officials refused to allow minority organizations to help run voter-registration drives. This may not have been blatant discrimination, but it was clear that many local and state officials still considered voting a privilege and not a right.

The "Motor Voter" Law

From 1970 through the early 1990s, Congress considered a number of proposals aimed at eliminating the remaining hurdles to registration and voting. But these measures generally failed because senators and representatives in Washington tended to shy away from dictating how the states should run federal elections. Also, members of Congress were no doubt reluctant to change a system that had worked to get them elected. On top of this, party considerations came into play: Even today, not everyone wants an enlarged electorate.

In 1992, however, after a multi-year campaign by voter-registration reform advocates from such organizations as the League of Women Voters and the National Association for the Advancement of Colored People (NAACP), Congress finally passed a law making voter registration easier and more convenient. The National Voter Registration Act required states to allow citizens to apply to register to vote when they get their driver's licenses. The law also required states to offer mail-in voter registration and registration at offices offering public assistance. President Bill Clinton signed the bill into law in May 1993.

The National Voter Registration Act took effect in most states on January 1, 1995. By the time of the 1996 presidential election, the number of registered voters in the United States had reached an all-time high, comprising more than 76 percent of the voting-age population. According to the Federal Election Commission (FEC), the surge in registrations in 1995 and 1996 was primarily due to the motor voter law.

Voter Turnout: Turn-offs and Turn-ons

With more people eligible to vote and voter registration rates on the rise, you'd think that the percentage of Americans showing up at the polls would be higher than ever. But that's not the case.

HOW TO BOOST VOTER REGISTRATION

When the "Motor Voter" Act took effect in 1995, it became easier for citizens across the United States to register to vote. Not surprisingly, the percentage of eligible Americans who were registered hit an all-time high.

	1992	1996
# of Registered Voters	133.8 million	149.8 million
Percentage of Voting-Age Population	70.6 %	76.25 %

In fact, between the 1960s and the 1990s, there was a steady drop in voter turnout, defined as the percentage of the voting age population that voted in a given election.

In 1960, 63 percent of Americans voted in the election that sent John F. Kennedy to the White House. But in 1996, the long downward trend hit bottom when only 49 percent voted for Bill Clinton over Bob Dole.

Observers who were getting discouraged about U.S. voter participation were pleased to see that the turnout rebounded a bit in 2000, when over 50 percent voted. And in 2004, the upturn was even sharper, as more than 55 percent of the voting age population went to the polls.

The increase in turnout among young Americans was especially noticeable. Nearly five million more people ages 18 to 29 voted in 2004 than in 2000. Turnout was up from 42 to 51 percent, a very significant increase, especially considering that, in a typical election, young people have the lowest turnout rates of any age group.

Voter turnout varies a lot from state to state. Minnesota had the highest turnout in 2004 with 73 percent, followed by Wisconsin with 71 percent. At the low end were Hawaii with 44 percent and Texas with 46 percent.

In 2004 more than 55 percent of the voting age population went to the polls.

What are the reasons for the decline—and then the rebound—in voter turnout? Thomas Patterson, a professor at Harvard University, looked at factors that have depressed turnout in *The Vanishing Voter*, a thoughtful book published in 2002. Patterson pointed to a number of important factors that keep people away from the polls:

+ The campaign calendar—it starts before voters are ready to focus on the campaign and features a short rush of primaries, then a long inactive period before the party conventions
+ The growth of negative campaign advertising, which tends to turn off voters
+ Media coverage, which is often very critical, even cynical,

about politics and politicians. Like attack advertising, this approach discourages citizen participation in politics.

On top of all this, Patterson noted, a growing number of American residents—non-citizens, prison inmates, and convicted felons—are ineligible to vote. Roughly 10 percent of adult residents of the United States cannot vote, compared with 2 percent in Britain. An additional factor may well be advertising overload. By the time Election Day nears, many people have been exposed to hundreds of candidate ads, campaign mailings, and phone calls, and may get turned off to the election process.

Nearly five million more people ages 18 to 29 voted in 2004 than in 2000.

Low voter turnout rates are especially disappointing because a number of factors since 1972 would seem likely to boost turnout. Those factors include: a more educated electorate; African-American voters now able to vote throughout the United States; political competition in the South; and more voter-mobilization efforts by both parties and nonparty groups, such as the Christian Coalition and unions.

Turnout Rises in 2004

The significant rise in voter turnout in the 2004 presidential race, to more than 55 percent, probably had a number of reasons. One undoubtedly was the highly charged political atmosphere of that year. With the war in Iraq not going well, opponents of the Bush administration felt highly motivated to do all they could to elect a new president. At the same time, Republicans felt a strong obligation to rally around the president and the war effort. These factors may well play a role in keeping turnout relatively high in 2008.

In addition, rules defining when and where an American can vote are becoming more flexible. More states are permitting people to vote by absentee ballot, no questions asked, so that they can vote up to a month before the official Election Day. The leader in this trend is the state of Oregon, in which all voters are encouraged to vote by mail, though Oregonians who want to can still come down to a county elections office to vote in person. Some states also permit early voting at designated early polling places. It's estimated that in 2004, as many as ten million voters actually cast their ballots before the big day, November 2.

Another factor in improved turnout might well be a change in U.S. election law, which now guarantees all American voters the right to "provisional voting." Under the Help America Vote Act passed in 2002, if a person goes to vote but is not on the list of eligible voters, they still get to cast a ballot then and there. If it turns out that they are really eligible, their vote is counted. (Before this change, thousands of voters used to get turned away from the polls at every election.)

It's estimated that in 2004, as many as ten million voters actually cast their ballots before the big day, November 2.

In November 2004, approximately 1.9 million voters nationwide cast provisional ballots. Of those, approximately 1.2 million—or 64.5 percent—were counted. Chances are, many of those people would not have gotten to vote if it hadn't been for the new law.

In most other countries around the world, voter turnout rates are higher than in the United States. For example, according to the International Institute for Democracy and Electoral Assistance, in recent presidential elections 79 percent of the voting age population in Argentina actually voted, as did 78 percent in Costa Rica, 68 percent in Russia, 85 percent in Israel, 77 percent in Finland, and 64 percent in the Central African Republic. The United States did do better than Mali in North Africa, one of the poorest countries in the world, where only 29 percent voted.

Political scientists debate whether America's voter turnout is as bad as it looks. Some experts point out that the figures above show voters as a percentage of the "voting-age population," which includes noncitizens and convicted felons who cannot legally vote in most states. According to one expert, if you compute turnout rate based on the population legally eligible to vote rather than the voting-age population, the United States comes out with a more respectable turnout in 2004 of over 60 percent, rather than 55 percent.

VOTER TURNOUT IN
PRESIDENTIAL ELECTIONS, 1960-2004

Year	% of Voting-Age Population
1960	62.8
1964	61.4
1968	60.7
1972	55.1*
1976	53.6
1980	52.8
1984	53.3
1988	50.3
1992	55.2
1996	49.0
2000	50.3
2004	55.5

Source: Statistical Abstract of the United States

*A likely factor in the significant decline in voter turnout between 1968 and 1972 was the ratification of the Twenty-sixth Amendment to the Constitution in 1971. The amendment expanded the right to vote to younger Americans (18 to 21 years of age)—a group that historically has recorded low turnout rates when compared to other segments of the population.

Turning Things Around: How to Increase Voter Turnout

There are a number of possible responses to the decreasing voter turnout in the United States. Thomas Patterson, *author* of *The Vanishing Voter*, has suggested several concrete steps that could be taken, either to make it easier to vote or to make the political process more attractive to potential voters. For example, registering to vote is seen as a bureaucratic obstacle by many people who might be interested in voting. Seven states have adopted election-day registration, which means citizens can go to their polling place or county courthouse, register, and vote all at one time. In 2000, these states had a voter turnout 15 percent higher than other states. They generally rank among the states with the highest turnout in the nation.

As we noted above, allowing people to vote at times and places other than the traditional Election Day visit to the polling station generally helps turnout. As of May 2007, fifteen states offered voters the option of early voting with no need to give reasons why, and that number is gradually increasing.

In addition, civil rights and civil liberties groups advocate changing state laws to restore voting rights to convicted felons who have completed their sentences. They say that these citizens have, as the saying goes, "paid their debt to society" and should get back their full civil rights. One expert estimates that about three million U.S. citizens are prohibited from voting because they are "ineligible felons." The exclusion has a disproportionate impact on minority communities.

> *A completely different way of boosting voter participation might be to improve the content of American politics.*

Other conceivable changes in the framework or scheduling of elections might encourage voter participation—but some of these are reforms on a scale that would be difficult to implement. For example, Congress could change the campaign schedule so as to get rid of the long "dead period" between the primaries and the conventions. This might well keep voters more interested in the campaign. (However, the trend for 2008 is moving in the opposite direction—a big cluster of primaries in February, and then a very long wait until the conventions five or six months later.) Another approach might be to schedule elections less frequently, since some research indicates that "voter fatigue" lowers turnout.

Some argue that abolishing the Electoral College and moving to direct popular election of the president would increase the vote—since all citizens would have a vote that counted equally in the final result. (With the Electoral College system, votes are counted by state, so that voters who live in a state where one candidate is the odds-on favorite may feel that voting is meaningless.) Eliminating the Electoral College, however, would require an amendment to the U.S. Constitution and is very unlikely.

People need information that connects the election to what's happening at work, in their communities, and in their homes.

A completely different way of boosting voter participation might be to improve the content of American politics—that is, to get the candidates and the political parties to focus more on the issues and less on the scripted, feel-good events and the negative appeals that dominate today's national political campaigns. But many people believe that major changes in the way political campaigns are run in the United States are about as likely as a comet striking Chicago. If this is true, perhaps the best way to boost turnout is to make sure voters have as much information as possible about the candidates and the issues and about how the election will affect people's lives.

According to the League of Women Voters' own research, the degree to which people feel that the outcome of an election will affect them and their families has a lot to do with whether or not they vote. In other words, people need information that connects the election to what's happening at work, in their communities, and in their homes.

Getting election information has become a lot easier in recent years, thanks in great part to the Internet. But that doesn't mean the rest of the media are off the hook. In fact, many people believe newspapers, radio, and television can do a much better job of reporting on the issues and informing voters about what's at stake in elections (see chapter 4 on the media).

Yet another way to increase voter turnout is for citizens to become involved in encouraging friends, family members, and coworkers to vote.

For example, a Harvard University survey taken just after the 2004 election showed that for 61 percent of first-time voters, having family members or friends encouraging the person to vote was a big factor in getting them to the polls. On the other hand, 20 percent of the people surveyed who did not vote in 2004 said they didn't have a way to get to the polls.

Results like these show that we each have the ability to increase voter turnout in this country. How can you help?

- Talk to people about the candidates and the issues and why you feel it's important to vote.
- Find out if your family, friends, and neighbors have what they need to make an informed decision and get to the polls. Maybe all they need is a ride.
- Don't go to the polling place alone. Make a date to take a friend.

A country where just over half the voting-age population is counted on Election Day clearly can and should do a better job of involving citizens in our democratic process. Do your part to help get out the vote!

The Debate Over Voter ID

You might guess that measures to increase voter turnout, such as making it easier to register, would be universally popular, but that's not the case. Over the past 20 years, laws such as the "motor voter" bill have gotten caught up in partisan controversy.

Some groups, including the League of Women Voters, have tried to make sure that it is easy to vote, while other groups have expressed concerns that unless rules are strictly enforced, voter fraud can occur. Their greatest concern is that felons or non-citizens might vote, when they are not legally entitled to do so.

Do your part to help get out the vote!

On a practical level, the question often comes down to whether would-be voters will have to show official ID in order to vote. While middle class people may assume that every American has a driver's license or similar government-issued ID, that's actually not the case.

REGISTER TO VOTE! IT'S EASIER THAN EVER

The National Voter Registration Act (aka motor voter) made registering to vote easier and more convenient. Now almost all states*must allow citizens to register to vote by mail and must accept a universal mail-in voter registration form designed by the Federal Election Commission. The form makes voter registration an easy, three-step process:

1. Get a mail-in voter registration form by calling your election office or the local League of Women Voters.
2. Complete the form according to the easy-to-follow instructions.
3. Mail the form to the address provided in the instructions.

The election office will notify you when your application has been approved and tell you where to go on Election Day to cast your ballot.

How else can you register? If you have Internet access, log on to the League's VOTE411 Web site, www.VOTE411.org. Click on "Register to Vote," then fill out the voter registration form that appears. Print it out and mail it in—the form has instructions on where to mail it.

*Eight states—Minnesota, Montana, North Dakota, Wyoming, Wisconsin, Idaho, Maine, and New Hampshire—are exempt from the "motor voter" requirements. That's because they either allow voters to register at the polls on Election Day or—in the sole case of North Dakota—don't require registration.

Under the motor voter law, many public agencies are supposed to have voter registration applications available. These include motor vehicles offices, public assistance offices (such as welfare and food stamps), and agencies that help people with disabilities. Registration forms can often be found in other public buildings as well, such as libraries and schools.

A recent study by the secretary of state of Georgia reported that nearly 700,000 of Georgia's registered voters did not have either a driver's license or a state-issued ID. This is consistent with figures from the U.S. Department of Transportation estimating that 6 to 12 percent of voters nationally do not have government-issued photo ID. One contributing factor: People who were born outside of hospitals may face problems in getting birth certificates or other proof of citizenship.

The nation is best served when voting rules are interpreted to help Americans vote, rather than to put barriers in the path of voting.

Studies show that people of color, seniors, young people, and poor people are less likely to have official identification. So those are the people most likely to be disqualified by strict voter ID rules.

In fact, a study of voter turnout during the 2004 election showed that in states that required ID at the polls, voters overall were 2.7 percent less likely to vote than in states where no ID was required. But the requirement had more impact on minorities: Latinos were 10 percent less likely to vote, African-Americans 5.7 percent less likely, and Asian Americans 8.5 percent less likely, according to research by the Eagleton Institute of Politics at Rutgers University.

On occasion, the tussle over voter ID has taken on a partisan tone, with Republicans more likely to advocate requiring proof of citizenship to prevent voter fraud, and Democrats more likely to advocate traditional procedures under which most people can vote by stating their name and address and signing the rolls. Both parties seem to believe that deciding who is permitted to vote may also determine the outcome of some close races.

The League of Women Voters holds that voter fraud is very rare and that the nation is best served when voting rules are interpreted to help Americans vote, rather than to put barriers in the path of voting.

CHAPTER 2

The Candidates

The candidates, of course, are the star players in the presidential election. They get all the attention, and they select the issues they'll focus on and the messages they'll convey to voters. They also determine how their campaigns will be run—though the candidate's campaign managers, pollsters, and other advisers usually play major roles in these decisions. How they'll go about their fund-raising, how many debates they'll participate in, how they'll work the Internet, whether they'll "go negative" in their advertising, and how much information they'll provide about their policy positions: These are all aspects of the campaign the candidate must address.

At the time this book was written, in mid-2007, both the Democratic and Republican fields appeared to be wide open. Because the Constitution prohibits a president from serving for more than two full terms, George W. Bush could not run for the office again. And Vice President Dick Cheney had stated from the beginning that he was not interested in running for president. So with no obvious successor to the president, a number of Republicans declared their candidacies. The leading contenders, with the most money in their treasuries and the strongest early poll numbers, were Senator John McCain of Arizona, former Massachusetts Governor Mitt Romney, and former New York City Mayor Rudolph Giuliani.

The Democrats—hoping to reoccupy the White House after eight years with President Bush—were also looking over a large number of declared candidates. The strongest candidates in mid-2007 appeared to be New York Senator (and former first lady) Hillary Rodham Clinton, Illinois Senator Barack Obama, and former North Carolina Senator and 2004 vice presidential candidate John Edwards.

In mid-2007, Republican Party activists found themselves in the unusual situation of not having a leading candidate from the conservative wing of their party who had close ties to the religious right. (Presidents Ronald Reagan and George W. Bush were successful candidates with those connections.) In fact, a Gallup poll in the spring of 2007 showed that only six out of ten Republicans were satisfied with their party's candidates, compared with eight out of ten Democrats who were satisfied with their party's offerings. The absence of a strong conservative candidate was seen as providing an opening for new candidates to enter the Republican race.

A Gallup poll in the spring of 2007 showed that only six out of ten Republicans were satisfied with their party's candidates, compared with eight out of ten Democrats who were satisfied with their party's offerings.

Are They Crazy? What It Takes to Run for President

A lot of people think that running for president today is a crazy thing to do. Not only must candidates raise tens of millions of dollars in contributions just to be contenders, but they have to give up normal life for month after month of nonstop campaigning that can start more than a year before the first primary. In addition, by entering a presidential race, candidates and their families are exposed to an extraordinary level of scrutiny that can turn personal and family matters into headline stories and can make past transgressions, however slight, into fodder for the opposition's negative advertising.

Sometimes strong potential candidates take themselves out of the race for these kinds of personal reasons, or because they don't feel the potential reward is worth the extraordinary stress and effort.

THE PRESIDENT: A POWERFUL CEO

One reason so many Americans are attracted to the presidency is that the Constitution, from the earliest days of the republic, set up a system of government with a strong chief executive officer. Article II of the Constitution, titled "Duties and Powers of the President," gives the president a job description that includes the following:

- Commander in chief of the Army and Navy, and of the militia (National Guard) when the guard is called up for federal service;
- Can grant pardons and reprieves;
- Can appoint judges of the Supreme Court and other federal courts, ambassadors, and other high U.S. officials, with the "advice and consent" of the Senate;
- Can veto legislation passed by Congress* (though a two-thirds vote of both the House and Senate can override a veto);
- Can make treaties, with the consent of two-thirds of the Senate;
- Shall report to Congress on "the State of the Union" and recommend laws for Congress to consider;
- "Shall take care that the laws be faithfully executed."

Beyond these official powers named by the Constitution, the president in fact has other important powers, including being head of his or her political party, and being the spokesperson for the country, which gives the president a great deal of media exposure and informal influence over the nation's political agenda.

*Note: the veto power is described in Article I of the Constitution.

The number and variety of candidates who are vying for the presidency in 2008, however, prove that for many, the attractions of serving in the White House still trump concerns about mounting a campaign to get there. A combination of personal drive and the desire to serve the country and see one's policies in place still makes the job of president of the United States an irresistible career move for many people both inside and outside of politics.

Where Do They Come From? The Candidates' Varied Backgrounds

Where do these people come from—these individuals who feel themselves qualified to lead their country and, in a sense, the world? More often than not, they come from other elective offices—governorships, the U.S. Senate, the House of Representatives—where they have shown they can appeal to voters and where they have built a public record of decision making and action on a variety of policy issues. Because American politics has been dominated by white men for so long, women and minority candidates for the presidency have been few and far between. Notable exceptions include Democrat Jesse Jackson in 1984 and 1988, Republican Elizabeth Dole in 2000, and in the 2004 election, the Reverend Al Sharpton and Carol Mosely-Braun.

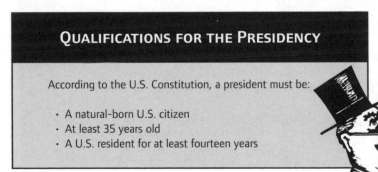

QUALIFICATIONS FOR THE PRESIDENCY

According to the U.S. Constitution, a president must be:

- A natural-born U.S. citizen
- At least 35 years old
- A U.S. resident for at least fourteen years

In the 2008 contest, however, the long-established expectations about who can be a serious contender for the presidency seem to be breaking down. As we've noted, among the strongest Democratic candidates are Hillary Clinton, a woman, and Barack Obama, an African-American. In addition, the Republican field includes Mitt Romney, a Mormon, which may indicate that the American public is becoming more open to a president with a non-traditional religious background.

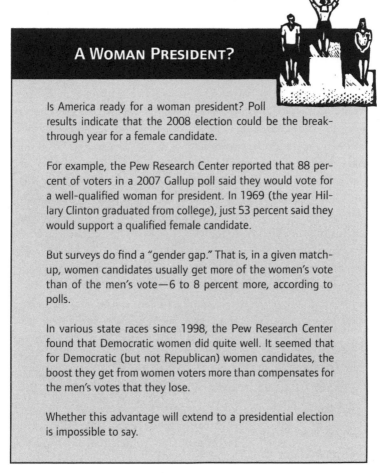

A WOMAN PRESIDENT?

Is America ready for a woman president? Poll results indicate that the 2008 election could be the breakthrough year for a female candidate.

For example, the Pew Research Center reported that 88 percent of voters in a 2007 Gallup poll said they would vote for a well-qualified woman for president. In 1969 (the year Hillary Clinton graduated from college), just 53 percent said they would support a qualified female candidate.

But surveys do find a "gender gap." That is, in a given match-up, women candidates usually get more of the women's vote than of the men's vote—6 to 8 percent more, according to polls.

In various state races since 1998, the Pew Research Center found that Democratic women did quite well. It seemed that for Democratic (but not Republican) women candidates, the boost they get from women voters more than compensates for the men's votes that they lose.

Whether this advantage will extend to a presidential election is impossible to say.

For many years, Congress—and, more specifically, the Senate—was considered the best launching pad for a presidential campaign. The power, the prestige, and the national visibility of a position in Washington, combined with experience dealing with issues from the federal budget to international affairs, made serving in the Senate good preparation if you had presidential ambitions.

In the 2008 contest, the long-established expectations about who can be a serious contender for the presidency seem to be breaking down.

On the Democratic side, nominees who served in the Senate at one time or another include John F. Kennedy, Hubert Humphrey, George McGovern, Walter Mondale, Al Gore, and John Kerry. Among Republicans, Barry Goldwater, Richard Nixon, and Robert Dole all served in the Senate before launching their presidential bids. Nixon and Gore had also served as vice president.

Over the last several decades, however, the Senate has given way to the governors' mansions as the odds-on source of successful presidential candidates. Four of the last five presidents—Carter, Reagan, Clinton, and George W. Bush—were governors before serving in Washington. In fact, John F. Kennedy in 1960 was the last serving senator to move directly to the White House. There may also be an element of luck in this pattern: In 2000, Senator John McCain and former Senator Bill Bradley both ran strong (though losing) campaigns for their parties' nominations.

With the United States at war in both Iraq and Afghanistan, perhaps the foreign policy expertise that can best be acquired in Washington will make a comeback as an important qualification for the presidency.

One often cited reason for the recent influx of former governors is the American public's well-documented disillusionment with Washington in the wake of the Vietnam era and the Watergate scandal in the 1970s. According to this theory, the public grew wary of candidates who had made their names in the nation's capital. Another factor people point to is that international issues were of less importance to voters in the post-Cold War 1990s. But after the September 11, 2001, terrorist attacks on the World Trade Center and the Pentagon, the United States faces a new set of challenges. With the United States at war in both Iraq and Afghanistan, perhaps the foreign policy expertise that can best be acquired in Washington will make a comeback as an important qualification for the presidency.

Even if it does, governors will still offer voters their real-world experience dealing with key domestic concerns, from education and the environment to balancing budgets and reforming welfare. They also offer very relevant expertise in managing large bureaucracies and dealing with legislatures.

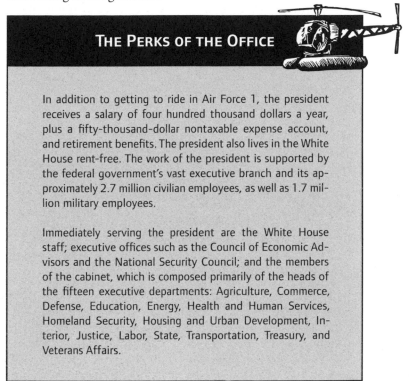

THE PERKS OF THE OFFICE

In addition to getting to ride in Air Force 1, the president receives a salary of four hundred thousand dollars a year, plus a fifty-thousand-dollar nontaxable expense account, and retirement benefits. The president also lives in the White House rent-free. The work of the president is supported by the federal government's vast executive branch and its approximately 2.7 million civilian employees, as well as 1.7 million military employees.

Immediately serving the president are the White House staff; executive offices such as the Council of Economic Advisors and the National Security Council; and the members of the cabinet, which is composed primarily of the heads of the fifteen executive departments: Agriculture, Commerce, Defense, Education, Energy, Health and Human Services, Homeland Security, Housing and Urban Development, Interior, Justice, Labor, State, Transportation, Treasury, and Veterans Affairs.

Running for the Boss's Job: When the Vice President Steps Up

Of course, not all presidential candidates come from the Senate or governorships. The vice presidency is considered an excellent stepping-stone to the nation's highest elective office—and not just because the vice president is first in line for the job if something should happen to the president. The office of the vice presidency offers a candidate the national visibility, staff resources, and nationwide contacts he or she needs within the party to lay the groundwork for a successful run for the presidential nomination. Moving directly from the vice presidency to the presidency, however, is not as easy as it might sound. Al Gore found this out in 2000, when he lost to George W. Bush. So did Richard Nixon, who had served as

Dwight Eisenhower's vice president for eight years and then lost to John F. Kennedy. In fact, in the past hundred years, the only sitting vice president to be elected president was George H. W. Bush (the first President Bush), who defeated Michael Dukakis in 1988. Nixon did ascend to the presidency, but only after eight years out of office.

Most of the former vice presidents who won election as president did it by first serving out the remainder of their predecessor's term when that president died in office. Presidents who came up by this route include Lyndon Johnson, Harry Truman, Calvin Coolidge, and Theodore Roosevelt.

> *One possible drawback of a vice president running for president is that the VP is associated, for better or worse, with the record of the president whom he or she served.*

One possible drawback of a vice president running for president is that the VP is associated, for better or worse, with the record of the president whom he or she served. This means opponents are often able to associate a sitting vice president in the public's mind with the controversies and the unpopular policies of the current administration, though being associated with a popular president will help a candidate. More importantly, during the campaign the vice president must walk a fine line. The VP must emerge from under the shadow of the president—must appear

THE LINE OF SUCCESSION

In the event that the president dies or is unable to serve out his or her term in office, Congress established a line of succession as follows: vice president; speaker of the House of Representatives; president pro tempore of the Senate; and the president's cabinet members in the order in which their departments were created, starting with the secretary of state. Never in the country's history has the line of succession passed below the vice president.

independent but also respectful of the president. That's not an easy trick to pull off.

Political Newcomers: Nonpoliticians in the Running

Does a presidential candidate have to have a record in elective office? No. Some presidential candidates have never won election to any public office, but enter the contest with other experiences that they and their supporters feel are qualification enough for the job. President Dwight Eisenhower, for example, rose to fame as supreme commander of the Allied forces in Europe during World War II.

More recent presidential aspirants who had never served in elective office but who entered the race with other experiences include: Jesse Jackson (civil rights activist); Ross Perot (computer company executive); Elizabeth Dole (former American Red Cross president and U.S. cabinet secretary); and Wesley Clark (Army general).

With the exception of military leaders, it is rare for someone without experience in public office to win the nomination of a major party.

With the exception of military leaders, it is rare for someone without experience in public office to win the nomination of a major party.

For both candidates with traditional political résumés and those who've never held office, it can be helpful to have a history of outstanding accomplishment in some nonpolitical arena. John McCain, for example, survived a grueling stint as a prisoner of war in Vietnam, and Bill Bradley had been a star NBA basketball player. Credentials such as these helped convince many in the media and the public in 2000 that these candidates had the character to be a good president.

Campaign Strategy, Part I: The Candidates and the Issues

Deciding what issues to focus on—and how to do that—is a major decision for the candidates as they weigh how best to connect with American voters. To be taken seriously by the media and the public, candidates need to define in simple terms why they are running and project ideas that connect with key concerns of the electorate. Many candidates, in fact, select just one or two high-profile issues that will differentiate them from the other contenders in their party. Standing out is key in the early going, when a candidate may face ten or more possible competitors for the party's nomination. In the 1996 contest for the Republican nomination, Steve Forbes set himself apart from his opponents by advocating a "flat tax" that would establish one low tax rate for all Americans. One of his opponents, broadcast commentator and former White House speechwriter Pat Buchanan, chose the issue of U.S. jobs going overseas; Buchanan's remedy was higher tariffs on imported goods.

More often than not, unique or unusual proposals such as Buchanan's and Forbes's are crafted as much to attract attention to the candidate as to provide a preview of how he or she would govern. After all, any major policy proposal that a presidential candidate suggests would require the support of the Congress after the election. And the more dramatic or radical the proposal, the less likely it is that Congress will agree to it.

As a result, these sorts of far-reaching ideas should be thought of as a candidate's neon signs. They beckon you in so you can check out the candidate and what he or she stands for. When the final platform is hammered out at the party convention, most of the more extreme ideological statements are usually removed or softened at the request of the party.

Campaign Strategy, Part II: Dividing the Electorate

Similarly, many candidates seek to differentiate themselves by making direct appeals to specific segments of the party faithful. On the Republican side, individual candidates often battle for the support of the Christian right by staking out hard-line positions on issues such as abortion and same-sex marriage. Recent examples of such candidates include Christian broadcaster Pat Robertson and, in the 2000 race, Gary Bauer, the former head of the Family Research Council, a conservative advocacy group.

On the Democratic side, there is often an early fight to gain the support of the most liberal wing of the party. Democrats who have positioned themselves as the "progressive candidate" in recent elections included Jesse Jackson in the 1980s. In 2004, Representative Dennis Kucinich and former Vermont Governor Howard Dean both appealed to the left wing of the party by taking strong stands against the Iraq war.

WHO PROTECTS THE CANDIDATES?

The U.S. Secret Service assumed full-time responsibility for protection of the president after the assassination of President William McKinley in 1901. Presidential aspirants were not offered this security option until sixty-seven years later, when Senator Robert F. Kennedy was shot while campaigning for the Democratic nomination for president. After Kennedy's assassination, President Lyndon Johnson issued an executive order calling for protection of all announced major candidates for the presidency. Johnson's order later became law, with the provision that candidates could decline protection.

Today, a five-person advisory committee determines whether prospective candidates meet the criteria for Secret Service protection.
To qualify, a candidate must:

- Be a declared candidate
- Have received financial contributions and be likely to qualify for federal matching funds
- Conduct an active campaign

The Secret Service has been known to make exceptions to these criteria. In 1979, for example, Senator Edward Kennedy was given Secret Service protection, even though he had not formally declared his candidacy for president.

Often, the candidates making these targeted appeals understand from the start that they have very little hope of winning the presidency. Instead, their goal is to introduce their issues into the campaign, to demonstrate support for their ideas, and, hopefully, to have some influence on the party's stands during the general election campaign and beyond.

The front-running candidates in both parties, by contrast, rarely propose controversial goals or policies that might alienate significant portions of their party's voters and prove a liability during the general election. Rather, the front-runners' goal during the early going and beyond is to get the mainstream of the party behind them as consensus candidates and to demonstrate "electability," or the ability to attract the support of the majority of American voters—Democrats, Republicans, and independents alike—come November.

CHAPTER 3

The Parties and Other Behind-the-Scenes Powers

The challenge of running a competitive campaign for the U.S. presidency is made easier by the existence of the political parties and other organizations—from the Sierra Club to the National Rifle Association—that support individual candidates and their agendas. The Democratic and Republican parties sponsor political advertising, organize volunteers, and help get out the vote on Election Day.

Before the 2004 election, some politicians and observers thought that the Democratic and Republican parties might be coming into a period of decline. That's because a campaign finance law passed in 2002—the Bipartisan Campaign Reform Act (BCRA, pronounced BICK-ruh)—was expected to put a big dent in how much money the parties could raise. The new law prohibited the parties from accepting "soft" money—that's the term for unregulated money with no limits on amounts. Instead, they'd have to raise all their funds in "hard" money, which is regulated by federal law. If they could no longer receive $100,000 checks from rich friends, would the parties survive?

As it turns out, they did just fine. In the years since BCRA passed, the parties mobilized and raised millions of dollars in hard money from small and medium donors and wound up with more money than ever before. Having weathered that storm, the two major parties are still enormously important players in presidential elections.

Early History: How the Political Parties Came to Be
     The U.S. Constitution has nothing to say about political parties. In fact, the Constitution's framers were resolutely opposed to the formation of political parties in this country. Based on their knowledge of the way things worked in Britain, the framers believed that parties created unnecessary and counterproductive divisions within a nation. They thought that candidates should be judged on their personal merits and their stands on the issues, not their party affiliations.

The Constitution's framers were resolutely opposed to the formation of political parties in this country.

     Before long, however, early opposition gave way to the political and practical convenience of a party system. Parties enhanced cooperation between the executive and legislative branches of government and made it easier to coordinate policy-making among the different levels of government—from the federal level down to the states, counties, and towns. More important, parties allowed diverse groups of like-minded Americans from throughout the country to come together and have an influence on national policy-making and the election of the president.

     Every individual elected to the U.S. presidency since George Washington has run with the support of one of the two major political parties of the time.

The Life of the Parties: The Democrats and Republicans Take Center Stage
     From the beginning, American politics has been dominated by two major parties. However, the constituencies and the names of these parties changed during the early years of the republic. The Democratic-Republicans of the Jefferson era were succeeded by the Democrats of President Andrew Jackson's time. The Federalists, who came together during George Washington's presidency, in time became the Whigs, who were eventually incorporated with other groups into the Republican Party under President Lincoln.

     How have the parties' constituencies changed? Many observers note that in recent years, the Republican Party has become increasingly conservative. Although there is a range of opinion within the party, Republicans generally advocate a limited role for the federal government in solving society's ills. Republicans also tend to support lower taxes, cuts in a range of domestic programs from social welfare to environmental protection, and increases in spending for defense. They also tend to oppose abortion rights and gun control.

Every individual elected to the U.S. presidency since George Washington has run with the support of one of the two major political parties of the time.

Under President George W. Bush, the Republican Party has not been doctrinaire about reducing the size of government. For example, the party succeeded in adding a major new benefit, drug coverage, to the Medicare program for seniors. Republicans also strongly supported going to war in Iraq and Afghanistan after the terrorist attacks of September 11, 2001—in line with the party's usual support for a robust military.

Despite its origins in the anti-slavery movement of the 1850s, the Republican Party has over the last half century achieved important electoral gains in the South. Some trace the Republican transition to Democratic President Lyndon Johnson's embrace in the 1960s of the traditional Republican cause of civil rights, a move that drove conservative Democrats—many of them from the South—into Republican ranks. Republicans also adopted a "Southern strategy" to welcome into the party Southern whites alienated by Democrats' support for civil rights and other liberal policies.

This realignment also convinced most African Americans to shift their allegiance from the Republican to the Democratic Party. While black Americans had once predominantly preferred the "party of Lincoln," by the 1970s most were reliable supporters of Democratic candidates, and still are.

The Democrats have been identified since the 1930s as the more progressive party, thanks in large part to Democratic President Franklin Roosevelt's New Deal programs, designed to alleviate problems caused by the Great Depression. Roosevelt's programs converted large numbers of progressive Republicans into progressive Democrats and laid the foundation for ideological battles about the role of the government in solving problems that continue to this day. In the late 1960s and 1970s, the Democratic Party, influenced by the civil rights movement, the anti-Vietnam War movement, and other social movements, shifted noticeably to the left.

THE PROS AND CONS OF THE TWO-PARTY SYSTEM

PROS

The Parties Help Voters Decide
They help clarify the issues and simplify the choices voters have to make in elections. Without the parties, voters would have to find their way through a confusing maze of issues and candidate positions with little help. With parties, government can be held accountable—if you don't like how Party A is running your city, you have a definite alternative to vote for.

The Parties Make Government More Effective
Parties are often the link among the different branches of the U.S. government and the three levels of government—federal, state, and local. They enable politicians to form coalitions and to get things done.

The Parties Make It Easier to Run for Office
Just as parties help the voters, they help candidates by providing an existing base of support and mobilizing voters and party supporters behind a candidacy.

CONS

The Parties Limit the Choices for Voters
Because we have only two dominant parties, the parties generally select candidates with the broadest possible appeal. The system discourages campaigning by "fringe" or even remotely controversial candidates.

The Parties Promote Division and Deadlock
Each party is forever seeking political advantage over the other. As a result, candidates and sitting officeholders are under pressure to stick to the "party line" and not to compromise with the other party. This hyper-competitive attitude contributes to gridlock in Congress, preventing constructive solutions to complex and controversial issues.

The Parties Promote Corruption
Throughout the nation's history, the political parties have been associated with corrupt practices, such as patronage and the awarding of government contracts to party insiders— and those charges are still made today. In addition, the parties regularly face criticism for questionable fund-raising practices that effectively place politicians in debt to big contributors (see chapter 5 for more).

During the 1990s, the Democratic Party under the leadership of President Bill Clinton moved toward the center of the American political spectrum. It adopted some policies that had traditionally been considered conservative, such as free trade, a balanced budget, and a smaller federal government. Nonetheless, the Democrats generally support a more active government role in protecting the environment, public education, and public health and in ensuring equal opportunity for all citizens. The party also tends to support abortion rights and some forms of gun control.

The Republican and Democratic Parties have regularly contested national elections in the United States since the Civil War. Today, most federal and state officeholders, and many local ones as well, are chosen on a partisan basis.

These days, the four core functions of the political parties are:

1. Raising money
2. Recruiting candidates
3. Mobilizing volunteers
4. Providing a message that will appeal to voters and help the party's candidates win election

Party Mechanics: How the Parties Work

The political parties are structured to reflect the U.S. political system, with party organizations at the national, state, and local levels.

The National Committees

Each of the major political parties is led by a national committee headquartered in Washington, D.C. While the national parties used to come to life only every four years in running the presidential nominating conventions, in the last three decades they have shifted dramatically to full-time professional organizations supporting state and local parties and recruiting and training candidates.

In addition to the Democratic National Committee (DNC) and the Republican National Committee (RNC), the two major parties each have official campaign committees that raise money to elect the parties' House and Senate candidates.

In recent election cycles, a key function of the Democratic and Republican National Committees has been to raise money to support its party and candidates. In 2004, the DNC took in $394 million and the RNC raised $392 million. (Interestingly, that was the first time since records have been kept that the DNC's receipts exceeded the RNC's, though overall the several Republican committees still beat the Democratic total.).

The amounts raised by the parties almost invariably increase from one election cycle to the next. (Campaign finance experts usually look at a two-year period, such as 2007–2008, as one "election cycle.") As we've mentioned, some experts thought that the campaign finance reform law of 2002 might reduce the parties' fundraising, but the parties adjusted to the new rules and have, in fact, continued to bring in more contributions.

Much of the money raised by the national party organizations is passed along to state and local parties to run their campaigns. Funds are also used to pay for advertising, consultants, direct mail campaigns, get-out-the-vote efforts, and many other activities.

Other important national committee tasks include planning the party's presidential nominating convention, promoting the election of party candidates at the national level, and trying to coordinate the work of the party at all levels—for example, by creating a unifying message for the party and its candidates.

The national committees are composed of two or more party representatives, including at least one man and one woman, from each state and U.S. territory; the Democrats also include representatives of other groups within the party, including members of Congress, Democratic governors, state and local officials, and party organizations for youth and women.

Appointment to the national committee is considered a high honor and is often a reward for years of service or financial support to the party and its candidates. Some states select national committee members at state party conventions; others select them by a vote of the state party committee; and still others put the selection of national committee members to voters in the party primary.

The chair of the national committee is usually an experienced politician or political professional. This person is elected by the national committee, but is often handpicked for the job by the president, or, if the party doesn't hold the presidency, by the party's presidential nominee or leading candidate for president. As the party's chief spokesperson and administrator, the chair oversees a staff of professionals and consultants in fundraising, communications, political organizing, and other specialties.

The State and Local Parties

The parties also have committees at the state and local levels throughout the country, which play an important role in a presidential campaign. They keep up enthusiasm at the grass roots, distribute campaign literature, and provide staff for candidates' headquarters and polling places.

Support from party leaders and volunteers at the state and local levels is considered crucial to the success of a presidential campaign. Not only can they help organize campaign events, but the state and local parties also keep national headquarters informed about the key issues affecting their states and communities and which individuals and organizations can help deliver votes.

State and local party organizations are also important financially, raising and spending hundreds of millions of dollars on a range of campaign activities from registering voters to TV advertising. Unlike the national parties, state parties can usually accept "soft money," if they spend it on state and local activities.

In addition to supporting the party's presidential candidates, the state committees work to recruit and support statewide candidates, develop a statewide issue agenda for the party, and coordinate the selection of delegates to the national party conventions.

County, city, and town committees recruit and support local candidates and coordinate "on-the-ground" activities, such as getting out the vote on Election Day.

Independents' Day: Beyond the Parties

The Democratic and Republican Parties have been the dominant political parties in the United States for more than a century, but for many years, a considerable number of Americans have called themselves independents. (See box, page 37.)

But what exactly is meant by an "independent"? The experts say that defining the independent voter is complicated. That's because many Americans who say they are independent also say that they generally feel closer to either the Republican or the Democratic Party. And political scientists say that independents who lean toward one of the major parties aren't fully independent—when it comes time to vote, they usually act a lot like Republicans or Democrats.

That may seem like a fine distinction—but it makes a big difference in how many independents we count. For example, according to the respected Stanford/University of Michigan American National Election Studies poll in 2004, 10 percent of Americans said they were independent and didn't prefer either major party. Another 17 percent said they were independent but leaning toward the Democrats, while 12 percent said they were independent but felt closer to the Republicans. So if you count only the independents with no party preference, 10 percent of the voting population is independent. If you count the "leaners" too, you find that 39 percent of the population is independent. That's an enormous difference. On the other hand, if you count the "leaners" as party affiliates, then 49 percent of Americans identified as Democrats or Democrat-leaning in 2004, while 41 percent identified as Republican or Republican-leaning.

PARTY IDENTIFICATION, 1964–2004

Year	Democrats	Republicans	Independents
1964	61%	30%	8%
1968	55%	33%	11%
1972	52%	34%	13%
1976	52%	33%	15%
1980	52%	33%	13%
1984	48%	39%	11%
1988	47%	41%	11%
1992	50%	38%	12%
1996	52%	38%	9%
2000	50%	37%	12%
2004	49%	41%	10%

Notes: These figures are based on polls asking which party a person identifies with—not voter registration. Independents leaning toward Democrats or Republicans are grouped with that party.

Source: American National Election Studies. See http://www.electionstudies.org/nesguide/toptable/tab2a_2.htm

According to the Pew Research Center on the People and the Press, the number of people surveyed who say they are Republican or Republican-leaning dropped several points between 2004 and 2007. It's likely that low approval ratings for President Bush and the increasingly unpopular war in Iraq contributed to that decline.

The number of independents has changed over time. Back in the 1950s, a mere 6 percent of Americans said they were independents.

This number grew in the 1960s and peaked in the 1970s—perhaps in response to the Vietnam War and the Watergate scandal, which alienated many people from "establishment" politics. Currently, younger adults are more likely than older Americans to identify as political independents.

The most vivid recent example of independent politics was the phenomenon of Ross Perot in the 1990s. In 1992, the billionaire businessman ran for president under the banner of an unusual political movement called United We Stand and attracted an unprecedented 19 percent of the popular vote. Nearly twenty million Americans chose Perot over the major-party candidates, Bill Clinton and George H. W. Bush. Four years later, he garnered only 8 percent of the vote under the banner of the Reform Party. Unlike third-party candidates who have usually run from the right or left of the political spectrum, Perot ran on an interesting set of issues that some called the "radical center." Among these issues were reducing the federal deficit, reducing the influence of big money in politics, and protecting American businesses and jobs from international competition.

Currently, younger adults are more likely than older Americans to identify as political independents.

Of course, only a very small fraction of elected officials at the national and state levels are unaffiliated with either the Democratic or the Republican Party. Out of 535 elected members of Congress in 2007, only two, Senator Joe Lieberman of Connecticut and Senator Bernie Sanders of Vermont, were independent.

The two major parties, while still very powerful, probably do not have as strong a hold on the loyalties of the American people as they did fifty or a hundred years ago. Why is this? One factor may be that in previous generations, politics was more of a face-to-face, grassroots activity. The parties had a unique capability to mobilize millions of people. These days, campaigns are largely run via the mass media. Candidates can appeal to voters directly without going through party organizations. In addition, since the 1970s, primaries have become the main method of nominating Democratic and Republican candidates, from the president on down. Primaries are much more democratic and open than party conventions, but they remove what used to be a key role of the party organization—choosing candidates.

PARTIES' SPENDING ON THE RISE

The Democratic and Republican Parties spend huge sums of money during every election cycle in the hope of influencing voters' decisions. During the 2004 campaign, the two major parties raised nearly $1.5 billion, spending much of it on the presidential and congressional races.

That was up from about $1.2 billion in 1999–2000. And that $1.5 billion doesn't include about $400 million that the state parties spent on candidates for Congress and president and millions more spent on state and local campaigns.

Party spending tends to peak every four years, during presidential elections, and drop off a bit during the mid-term election years like 2002 and 2006.

The money was provided by individuals, corporations, labor unions, political action committees, and other interest groups (see chapter 5 for more on the parties' fund-raising activities).

As mentioned above, some experts thought that overall party spending might drop in 2004 because of the campaign finance law known as BCRA, but that didn't happen. The upward trend just continued.

Enter the Special Interests: Independent Groups Step Up Their Campaign Activity

The political parties aren't the only organizations working to influence the outcome of American elections. Recent presidential and congressional races have seen groups such as the Christian Coalition, the AFL-CIO, the American Medical Association, and many others playing an increasingly important—and increasingly aggressive—role in promoting candidates and their ideas and getting Americans to the polls.

In addition, in recent elections, individuals and organizations with millions of dollars to spend have formed special committees to influence the outcome of the presidential and congressional races. In some cases, these groups are established under the law so that they can accept unlimited funds and may not have to reveal who their donors are. (See box: Groups that Influence Elections, page 41.) Some of these committees are violating the spirit of campaign finance laws—though they may be doing it entirely within the letter of the law.

Some of the wealthiest organizations have such generic names, like the Joint Victory Committee (a Democratic 527 committee) and Progress for America (Republican), that it's impossible to know what their goals are without doing some research.

Many advocates of campaign finance reform would like to see stricter rules governing these high-flying political committees, including making them subject to the same contribution limits as political action committees (or PACs), which are closely regulated by federal election law.

Many critics of the current system say that interest groups in the United States are exerting unprecedented influence on who is elected to national office.

Interest groups have found many ways to exert influence on the American political scene. Sometimes the groups directly help out in a favored candidate's campaign by donating money or volunteer labor. One of the most common tactics is to form political action committees (PACs), which are able to contribute to candidates more freely than corporations or unions can. Another common approach is called "bundling." That's when an individual or an organization asks many people to each donate money, which is then given in one nice package to the preferred candidate. An advocacy organization that can put together hundreds of thousands of dollars can generate real clout in the world of U.S. politics.

Many critics of the current system say that interest groups in the United States are exerting unprecedented influence on who

GROUPS THAT INFLUENCE ELECTIONS

Interest groups that seek to influence federal elections (that is, for president and Congress) have three main ways to organize themselves under U.S. election and tax law. Of the three, political action committees are the most heavily regulated, so individuals and interest groups that want to spend lots of cash on campaigns are increasingly making use of 527 and 501(c) groups.

POLITICAL ACTION COMMITTEES (PACs)—PACs are allowed to raise and spend only "hard" money that complies with strict federal regulations. PACs are limited in how much they can accept from donors and how much they can donate to any campaign, though they can spend unlimited amounts of their own money independently. PACs must report who their large donors are and how they've spent their money.

527 COMMITTEES—Organized under Section 527 of the Internal Revenue Code, they must report major donors to the IRS, but rules are less strict than for PACs. The biggest difference: 527s can accept unlimited donations of "soft," unregulated money. And in 2004, some 527s received millions from individual donors. During the 2004 campaign, one 527, Swiftboat Veterans for Truth, got lots of publicity when it aired questionable attacks on the war record of Democratic candidate John Kerry.

501(C) GROUPS—This section of the tax code used to cover mostly old-fashioned nonprofit groups like the American Red Cross, but in recent years, political players have discovered they can use this type of tax-exempt group to run political ads and engage in other similar activities. 501(c) groups do not have to reveal their donors or their expenditures. Such groups are not supposed to have political action as their primary purpose, but this rule is sometimes ignored.

is elected to national office. Although labor unions and corporations aren't allowed to donate directly to campaigns, they can and do organize political committees that can engage in a full range of activities. They also conduct their own outreach to voters through "independent expenditures" and "issue advocacy" advertising. Unions and other membership organizations have the added advantage of being able to mobilize their members to work for candidates they support.

Some interest groups have also focused considerable energy on supporting particular people to become delegates to the national conventions of the Democratic and Republican Parties. This strategy has been successful for labor unions, teachers organizations such as the National Education Association, and the Christian Coalition, which have elected their supporters or members as delegates. This way, the organizations can affect not only the choice of candidates, but also the parties' platforms on issues important to them.

BCRA, the Bipartisan Campaign Reform Act of 2002, placed new restrictions on what interest groups can do to help favored candidates, especially in the period just before Election Day. And in fact, the law did just that during the elections of 2004 and 2006. The law said that advocacy groups such as corporations and unions could not use their own funds to pay for television or radio ads that mention a candidate within sixty days of a general election or within thirty days of a primary.

The Supreme Court's 2007 ruling helps ensure that big money spending will continue to overpower voters' voices.

BCRA, also known as the McCain-Feingold Act, was upheld by the U.S. Supreme Court in 2003. But in a surprising turn of events, the Supreme Court — its composition now changed by the addition of two more conservative justices — reversed its stand on an important section of BCRA in June of 2007.

The more conservative Court ruled that the section of BCRA that prohibited corporations and unions from running radio and TV ads about candidates before an election was actually very questionable. Chief Justice John Roberts expressed concern that this part of BCRA might infringe on free speech, though the Court did not say outright that this section of the law was unconstitutional.

The League of Women Voters and other groups advocating clean elections and a reduced role for monied interests in the electoral process expressed grave disappointment in the Court's 2007 ruling. The decision "helps ensure that big money spending will continue to overpower voters' voices," the League said.

Independent Expenditures and Advocacy

Under current law, there are no limits to the amounts organizations such as PACs can spend on independent election activities designed to support a particular candidate, as long as these activities meet certain conditions:

1. They cannot be coordinated with the candidate's campaign
2. They must be paid for with federally regulated hard money
3. They must be reported to the Federal Election Commission

A major reason that organizations have this wide freedom of action is the Supreme Court decision in the case Buckley v. Valeo. The Court ruled in 1976 that money is the equivalent of communication in our society, and therefore any limitation on money will limit freedom of speech. A more recent minority opinion by Justice John Paul Stevens asserted that money "is property and not 'speech,'" but the Court has steadfastly held to its view and Congress has not been able to come up with a way around it.

Independent organizations spent over $300 million on "issue advocacy" advertising during the 1999–2000 federal election cycle and will probably spend more in 2008. In practice, many of these ads didn't simply talk about issues—they often mentioned candidates for office, including presidential candidates (though some were genuine issue ads). As we've discussed above, rules about TV and radio advertising were stricter in 2004 and 2006 because of BCRA. But due to the 2007 Supreme Court decision that loosened the BCRA rules about advertising, interest groups will be able to help candidates they favor with fewer restrictions in 2008.

In addition to independent organizations, the Democratic and Republican Parties spend lots of money on issue ads. According to the Annenberg Public Policy Center at the University of Pennsylvania, the Democrats at all levels spent more than $78 million dollars in 1999–2000, while the Republicans spent more than $83 million. Those figures were undoubtedly higher in 2004 and will be still higher in 2008.

Among the most important interest groups are business groups and labor unions. Business groups, some of them drawn from one specific industry, are often able to raise and distribute large sums of money. Labor generally is unable to generate as much money as the business sector, but the unions can also mobilize members to volunteer for campaigns, which increases their clout. However, union membership in the United States has steadily declined since its peak in the mid-twentieth century, which has lessened labor's political influence. Labor tends to give almost entirely to Democrats. Business groups give to both major parties, but tend to favor the Republicans.

One trend that has unfortunately become common is for interest groups to hide their identity behind innocuous-sounding names, so that their advertising is more palatable to the public. For example, the U.S. pharmaceuticals industry—a very big spender on issue advertising—uses such names as "Citizens for Better Medicare," or "United Seniors" in its ads. There are good reasons for ploys like this: A 2002 poll indicated that 58 percent of respondents had an unfavorable view of pharmaceuticals companies, while only 5 percent had an unfavorable view of "United Seniors."

When ads from disguised interests appear on TV and radio, it may result in confusion for voters, who often can't figure out who's paying for what commercials—and why. Voters can have a hard time distinguishing legitimate campaign advertising from the narrow and often negative appeals of independent, single-issue organizations. These independent ads also make it hard for voters to hold candidates accountable for statements made on their behalf. The candidates can claim that the attacks made on their opponents are not made by their campaigns.

WHO'S SPONSORING THAT AD?

As the presidential campaign season gets under way, television and radio ads will start appearing out of nowhere. Make sure to listen or watch until the end of the ad for the sponsor—and if it's not a candidate's campaign, take the whole thing with a grain of salt. It's probably an independent group with an ax to grind—or with a clear stake in how the election turns out.

If a radio or TV ad is paid for by a candidate's organization, it is required to have those familiar words, "My name is X and I approved this ad" (or something similar). That rule, passed as part of BCRA in 2002, is intended to make candidates and their campaigns more accountable for what their advertising says.

In heavily contested congressional races, or in states where there is a competitive presidential race, the amount of TV and radio advertising can become overwhelming for voters, and some may become alienated from the political process.

Also troubling, according to many observers, is that issue advocacy campaigns that help a candidate get elected can make that candidate beholden to the special interests who bankrolled the advertising blitz.

The organizations sponsoring issue advocacy commercials counter that they are merely exercising their constitutionally protected right to free speech. They also argue that their messages are designed to inform voters about important issues that the candidates are trying to avoid. In addition, they point out, interest groups of all descriptions have always been important players in the American political process.

CHAPTER 4

The Media

Broadcast television, radio news, and the mainstream newspapers and newsmagazines have enormous influence on the presidential election process. These pillars of the traditional media are still the sources from which the majority of Americans get most of their news and information about the candidates, the issues, and the election.

In recent years, however, Americans have become increasingly disenchanted with the traditional media and their dominant role in American politics. The public's distrust of traditional institutions—together with the advent of new technologies—has opened the door to new ways for voters to get their election information. From radio talk shows to the Internet and twenty-four-hour cable news channels, the "new media"—some of which are no longer that new anymore—offer a wide and growing assortment of options for tuning in, and are becoming increasingly popular as election information resources.

Americans have become increasingly disenchanted with the traditional media and their dominant role in American politics.

Over the last several years, blogs, viral marketing, e-mail outreach, and other vehicles for online information sharing have virtually changed the definition of "media" by democratizing the process and allowing everyday citizens to shape the making of the news. This has had an undeniable impact on the way campaigns are run. Increasingly, candidates, supporters, voters and the media from all over the world are able to respond instantaneously and cheaply to events as they happen. The concept of the "news cycle" has been eroded, while presidential campaigns have had to develop quicker, more flexible communications strategies.

Some of the nontraditional media, like C-SPAN and candidate Web sites, offer information directly from the candidates and campaigns. Others, such as talk radio, offer mostly opinion.

Running for Coverage: The Candidates and the Media

Despite the burgeoning competition, the traditional media are still enormously important, though every year their dominance fades a little more. Newspapers and network television still reach the largest audiences in the United States. A modern presidential campaign is as much a battle for favorable coverage in the mainstream news media as it is a battle for votes.

In the early going, for example, the major newspapers and the network news programs can virtually create a presidential front-runner by giving him or her valuable exposure or simply by identifying his or her candidacy as the one to beat. Most news outlets give the greatest coverage to candidates who have the most money (their own money plus campaign contributions), as well as the most favorable ratings in public opinion polls. How much coverage the candidates get during the campaign depends on how the candidates perform in the early phases of the contest for their party's nomination.

Most news outlets give the greatest coverage to candidates who have the most money as well as the most favorable ratings in public opinion polls.

While acceptance by the mainstream media as a "major candidate" is a crucial asset, a candidate can attract media attention and buzz by performing unexpectedly well. Democrat Howard Dean proved this in 2003. A former Vermont governor, Dean had at first been considered a long-shot candidate by pundits and reporters. But when, with the help of a new style of Internet campaign, he

NETWORKS AND NEWSPAPERS LOSE THE NEWS

As recently as 1990, the major television networks—ABC, CBS, and NBC—had a dominant role in delivering news to the American people. In 1992, the nightly network news shows with Dan Rather, Tom Brokaw, and Peter Jennings regularly reached 60 percent of the adult population. By 2006, that number had declined to 28 percent—cut by more than half.

Newspapers, the most traditional of the major media, faced the same trend. While 58 percent of people polled in 1994 said that they had read a newspaper in the last day, by 2006 that figure was down to 40 percent—and that counts people who read the paper on the Web. In addition, older Americans are much more likely to be newspaper readers than people in their 20s—a trend that has the newspapers very worried.

Local TV news and radio reach lots of people, and both of these news media have also lost viewers or listeners in the past ten years. Cable TV news, the most influential of the new media, has held steady in recent years. In 2006, it was regularly watched by 34 percent of Americans.

The Internet has become a major source of news: In 2000, 23 percent of Americans polled said they regularly got news online, but by 2006 that figure was up to 31 percent. People who log on typically spend less time with their online news sources than people spend with newspapers, TV, or radio news. And while young people used to be the main consumers of news via the Internet, that's no longer true. Now people ages 50 to 64 are just as likely to get news on the Internet as those in their late teens and early 20s.

Source: Pew Research Center for the People and the Press, 2006 Media Consumption Survey.

began to attract excitement and donations, especially from young supporters dubbed "Deaniacs," journalists quickly changed the tone of their coverage. And when Dean, in the third quarter of 2003, broke Democratic fund-raising records, the media quickly labeled the former long-shot the new front-runner. On the other hand, when the candidate stumbled in 2004, the same media were quick to brand him a hot-head who wasn't ready for the big leagues.

One lesson that may be drawn from this example is that the media (and the pollsters, pundits, and politicians whom journalists often quote as expert sources) may bring strong preconceptions to their campaign coverage, but they also like an exciting new story. The unexpected rise of a little-known governor, with his innovative tactics and youthful appeal, was a great story—the kind of story that attracts ratings and readers.

But even if a candidate doesn't have a flashy new campaign style, there are still plenty of well-known ways to draw favorable media attention. One time-tested technique is to stage events with "good visuals" for the television cameras and news photographers. These can include large crowds enthusiastically waving banners and American flags, or a dramatic backdrop that highlights some of the issues the candidate is talking about—for example, a pristine lake if the topic is the environment, or a factory if the candidate is addressing economic issues. Often, a simple meeting between the candidate and voters in a family living room or a local coffee shop is enough to convey the message that this is someone who cares about real people.

Granting exclusive interviews to reporters and news organizations is yet another way in which the candidates court the press. Often, candidates will try to bypass the national media by conducting interviews with local reporters, who, they think, may be less jaded and less likely to ask difficult questions. (This may no longer be true—recent studies show that local journalists also ask their share of embarrassing questions.) Candidates may also seek local news interviews in order to tailor their coverage in battleground states.

Thanks to today's telecommunications technologies, a presidential candidate can sit in a studio in Washington, or anywhere, and conduct back-to-back interviews with television or radio reporters throughout the country. These reporters, in turn, often jump at the chance to offer their viewers or listeners an "exclusive" with one of the contenders for the presidency.

The Media under Fire: What's Wrong with Today's Election Coverage?

Because of their huge influence on the process, the news media often come under fire for how they cover elections. Among the criticisms from voters and politicians alike:

- The media focus too little on the issues and too much on personalities and the horse-race aspects of elections—who's ahead and who's behind.
- The media have become obsessed with covering—and uncovering—scandals and embarrassing stories involving the nation's elected leaders and candidates for office.
- An entire "talk industry" has developed, with politics as its central focus. On cable news channels and radio talk shows, journalists, former government officials, and others routinely offer their analysis and opinions of the latest political goings-on. The discussions aren't necessarily designed to inform, but rather to draw viewers and listeners in so that advertisers will buy time on their shows. Often, this is best done by focusing on scandals and controversies.
- Broadcasters especially face the added charge that their political coverage rarely delves beneath the surface of the issues and instead relies on short "sound-bite" quotes that allow the candidates to avoid saying anything of substance. In 1968, the average television sound bite for a candidate was more than forty seconds. In 2000, it was less than eight seconds. Newspapers also have drastically reduced the length of quotations from candidates.

In 2000 the average sound bite for a candidate was less than eight seconds.

- Too much of the news on television is not really news at all—it's "soft news" about health and lifestyles, celebrities and scandals. News about important national and international issues, including electoral politics, gets shortchanged. Aside from the content of the news coverage, critics also point out that the TV networks and newspapers have greatly reduced the amount of coverage devoted to elections. On the network evening newscasts, time devoted to elections in 2000 was down nearly half from its 1992 level. (On the congressional and state office levels, the cutbacks are even more severe.) No wonder the new media are able to step in and fill the gap.

Responding to criticisms regarding content, many in the news media say they are merely reflecting reality in their campaign reporting. They report the "horse-race" because elections are contests. If they report that Candidate X is the front-runner and Candidate Y doesn't have a shot, it's because this is what pollsters, party insiders, and other experts are telling them; it isn't something the media make up.

In addition, the focus on personality over policy and on style over substance is driven in large part by what the media believe consumers want. The network news programs are in a constant struggle to increase their ratings, and they fear they'll lose viewers if they produce a ten-minute segment on Medicare reform. Journalists also worry that reporting on issues will result in charges of ideological bias. People rarely argue that coverage of candidate lapses is politically motivated.

> *The focus on personality over policy and on style over substance is driven in large part by what the media believe consumers want.*

The news executives may have a point regarding what to cover in campaigns. News stories on campaign gaffes get more attention from voters, are more accurately recalled, and are more widely discussed than stories about policy questions, said Thomas Patterson in his book *The Vanishing Voter*. But superficial or sensational media coverage changes the tone of American politics. In a 2000 poll, for example, 62 percent of respondents agreed with the statement, "Political campaigns today seem more like theater or entertainment than like something to be taken seriously."

The media also defend themselves by saying they are a convenient scapegoat for unsuccessful candidates seeking to explain their poor showing at the polls. During the 1992 election, for example, President George H. W. Bush and his supporters often claimed

HOW TO DECIPHER THE POLLS

During a presidential election race, the news media often become fixated not on the candidates' ideas or their campaigning, but on the latest poll results. Here are a few things to keep in mind as you sort through all the numbers:

- Who sponsored the poll? Special-interest organizations often sponsor polls that are designed to place their issues at the top of the list of voters' concerns. For example, in 2006, Children Now, a California pro-education group, commissioned a poll showing that most respondents wanted better-trained teachers and schools with higher standards. Nobody was surprised by the results.
- Who was surveyed? Was it all adults or just likely voters? All parents or parents of school-age kids? Such factors can have a dramatic impact on poll results.
- How were the questions worded? The exact wording of survey questions also can skew the results. For example, if people are asked what issues are important and then are given a list of just five issues to choose from, there's a real possibility that key issues will be left out.
- When was the survey conducted? A poll is a snapshot of people's opinions at a specific time. If one candidate is getting favorable attention in the news during the week of the poll, then the numbers are likely to reflect it.
- What is the margin of error? Typically, a reputable poll has a margin of error of 5 percent or less. Translation: If the margin of error is 5 percent and one candidate is ahead in the poll by 5 percent, then it's just as likely that the race is a dead heat.

The most important thing to remember about polls, however, is this: The only poll that matters is the official one on Election Day. There's no telling what will happen until the people vote.

that the media were giving the Republican candidate less favorable coverage than his opponent, Bill Clinton. "Annoy the Media. Vote for Bush" became a bumper-sticker slogan and rallying cry for the losing candidate's supporters.

The Media Respond: Is Political Coverage Getting Better?

Criticism of the media has had an effect, and it can be seen in how various media organizations have refined their approach to political and issue coverage in recent years. Here are some of the "refinements":

+ They still do their polling and horse-race coverage, but newspapers such as the *Washington Post*, the *New York Times*, and *USA Today* now publish detailed "ad watches," analyzing the validity of claims made in the candidates' radio and television ads.
+ A few newspapers give space for candidates' speeches "in their own words." And some radio, TV, and cable networks are providing free airtime for candidates to state their positions without journalists' commentary in the weeks leading up to elections.
+ In the 1990s, a movement called "civic journalism," or "community journalism," encouraged a number of local newspapers and broadcasters to pursue new ways to delve more deeply into issues of concern to the public. The rationale is that journalists are members of their communities and should take responsibility for helping find solutions to problems. Some media organizations have expanded their election coverage to include extensive comparisons of local, state, and federal candidates' stands on the issues.
+ The television networks now make a point of ignoring some of the "photo opportunities" staged by the candidates' campaigns and try harder to focus on the issues that distinguish one candidate from another.

These and other efforts to improve political reporting have not been sufficient to improve people's perceptions of the media, according to opinion surveys. In a Gallup poll conducted in September 2005, respondents were about evenly split among those who said they had "a great deal" or "a fair amount" of confidence that the principal news media reported the news fairly and accurately (50 percent), versus those who said they had "not very much" or "none at all" (49 percent). The number of respondents who say they trust the media fell sharply and steadily between 1972 and 2000. For print media, that number has stabilized since 2000, but for most TV and radio outlets, credibility has continued to drop.

In 2005, a significant number of those polled said the media were too liberal (46 percent), versus 37 percent who said they were "about right" and 16 percent who saw them as too conservative. Republicans were much more likely than Democrats to distrust the media and view them as too liberal.

The New Media: Expanding Election Coverage

Since the early 1990s, several new forms of media have entered the picture for voters who had become wary of the dominant role of the mainstream press in the nation's political life. The 1992 presidential election was the first to witness the rise as a political force of the "new media"—a catchall term that came to include everything from talk shows on TV and radio to cable television and the Internet.

In 2005, a significant number of those polled said the media were too liberal (46 percent), versus 37 percent who said they were "about right" and 16 percent who saw them as too conservative.

What was different about 1992? It was the year Bill Clinton appeared on TV playing the saxophone, the year CNN and C-SPAN proved once and for all that Americans have an appetite for twenty-four-hour news, and the year that presidential campaigns first experimented with using the Internet to communicate with voters.

Several of the new media allowed more direct interaction between the candidate and voters than newspapers or TV news, which typically have reporters mediating between the candidate and the audience, interpreting events. In the 1990s, Don Imus's irreverent, nationally syndicated radio program became a required stop for national politicians seeking to connect with voters. However, since Imus lost his high-profile program after making offensive on-air comments in 2007, that probably won't be true in 2008. Larry King, Rush Limbaugh, and Bill O'Reilly are just a few of the others who have become media stars with real political impact.

For the candidates and their campaigns, the new media offer an overwhelming number of ways to tailor messages and appeals to specific voter groups—for example, by appearing on Black Entertainment Television, by connecting with Limbaugh's thirteen million reliably conservative listeners, or by reaching out to younger voters on MTV.

New Media = More Choices for Voters

It is true that the new media offer voters choices besides the major newspapers and the broadcast networks, which almost used to have a lock on what the American people knew and when they knew it. But these new media actually differ greatly among themselves.

Among Americans who turn to the Internet for news, three Web sites dominate the field: MSNBC, Yahoo, and CNN. Other frequently visited sites are Google, AOL, and FOX News. It is worth noting that many of the Web news outlets are directly connected to the old media. Time Warner owns CNN. MSNBC, which is linked to NBC, often airs programming that is considered too specialized for the broadcast network.

It is worth noting that many of the Web news outlets are directly connected to the old media.

And Web sites directly linked to the TV networks and major newspapers—such as ABC, the *New York Times*, and *USA Today*—also get lots of hits.

The cable news networks—FOX, CNN, and MSNBC—feature a great deal of commentary and opinion on their cable programming. Much of this commentary is far more critical than that found on the broadcast networks and gives voters a wider range of opinion on policy debates and elections. FOX in particular is known for its distinctly conservative approach to both news and commentary.

But the distinction between cable and broadcast programming is shrinking. CNN, for example, went through a makeover in 2002 and began offering much less hard news and much more talk and soft-news features.

There is no question, though, that C-SPAN, which has expanded to two outlets in many markets, does provide unfiltered coverage not only of Congress, but also of presidential campaign events. The rise of C-SPAN and the World Wide Web has allowed Americans to witness for themselves such events as candidate stump speeches, press conferences, and congressional policy debates—events that were previously interpreted for the public by the press.

Just 4 percent of Americans in 2006 said they regularly read online blogs where people discuss news events.

At a time when the national TV news programs, newspapers, and weekly newsmagazines are giving the public shorter and shorter candidate sound bites, the new media have offered a more direct link to the candidates and more choices for public debate. The new media often allow the public to go deeper into the substance of election-year politics than the old media formats permit.

A new media presence that has gotten lots of attention in recent years is blogs, short for weblogs and known collectively as the blogosphere. Though they are much talked about, blogs actually have a relatively small reach in comparison to the major Web sites or more traditional media. According to the Pew Center on People and Press, just 4 percent of Americans in 2006 said they regularly read online blogs where people discuss news events, though for people 18 to 24, that figure increased to 9 percent. About the same numbers of Republicans, Democrats, and independents read news blogs regularly. While liberal and progressive blogs undoubtedly play a role in sharing information on the left side of the political spectrum, their impact is still relatively small compared to conservative outlets, such as talk radio and FOX News.

When candidates are given more than an eight-second sound bite, they can actually explain something about what they believe. Particularly on call-in shows, candidates are more likely to get questions about policy issues. When journalists do the questioning, on the other hand, questions about strategy, tactics, and viability tend to predominate.

The appeal of the new media lies not only in their content, but also in their 24/7 availability. The Internet in particular allows users to access the latest news whenever it is convenient for them, rather than at a set broadcast or printing time. For many, the convenience is as big a draw as the source of the information.

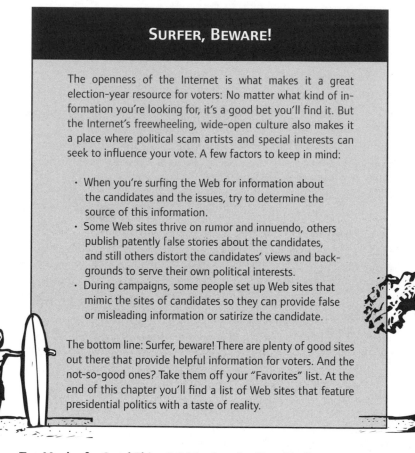

SURFER, BEWARE!

The openness of the Internet is what makes it a great election-year resource for voters: No matter what kind of information you're looking for, it's a good bet you'll find it. But the Internet's freewheeling, wide-open culture also makes it a place where political scam artists and special interests can seek to influence your vote. A few factors to keep in mind:

- When you're surfing the Web for information about the candidates and the issues, try to determine the source of this information.
- Some Web sites thrive on rumor and innuendo, others publish patently false stories about the candidates, and still others distort the candidates' views and backgrounds to serve their own political interests.
- During campaigns, some people set up Web sites that mimic the sites of candidates so they can provide false or misleading information or satirize the candidate.

The bottom line: Surfer, beware! There are plenty of good sites out there that provide helpful information for voters. And the not-so-good ones? Take them off your "Favorites" list. At the end of this chapter you'll find a list of Web sites that feature presidential politics with a taste of reality.

Too Much of a Good Thing? Critiquing the New Media

But the new media are not without their own critics. In particular, the emergence of talk shows such as CNN's Larry King Live, which one night might feature a Hollywood celebrity and the next a candidate for president has some people worried that journalistic standards are not being met. As *Newsweek* put it, "News, public affairs and history itself are morphing into entertainment."

And it does seem that the line between news and entertainment is becoming increasingly blurred. A poll released in 2004 by the Pew Research Center for the People and the Press found that 21 percent of Americans ages 18 to 29 cited "The Daily Show," which runs on the Comedy Channel, and "Saturday Night Live" as outlets where they regularly learned presidential campaign news. That's close to the 23 percent of young people who mentioned ABC, CBS or NBC's nightly news broadcasts as a source.

21 percent of Americans ages 18 to 29 cited "The Daily Show" and "Saturday Night Live" as outlets where they regularly learned presidential campaign news.

One concern is that television and radio talk shows—together with the speeches and campaign events carried uncut by C-SPAN or posted on the Internet—emphasize congeniality, glibness, and image over other qualities that Americans should be looking for in a president. And by providing an end run around seasoned political reporters, they allow candidates to avoid tough media scrutiny of their claims and ideas. Too often, the new media let the candidates control the discussion, though there are also hard-hitting and highly opinionated talk-show hosts who interrogate their guests mercilessly.

Another criticism is that the new media offer an illusion of direct communication with the candidates, rather than the real thing. It's not only a question of how many people get through to the talk shows to ask a candidate questions. It's also which callers get through. All talk shows have producers who screen callers. They select those who will be most entertaining for the talk-show host to speak to—either because the caller is a "ditto-head" or is someone the host can insult with impunity to the amusement of listeners. Most radio talk shows have a conservative political orientation.

To combat the predominance of conservative voices in talk radio, a group of liberals in 2004 launched a left-leaning talk radio network called Air America. But the network experienced financial difficulties early on and has not come close to achieving the ratings or influence of conservative radio programs.

It does seem that the rapid growth in popularity of talk radio may have ended. According to the Gallup Poll organization, talk radio expanded its daily listeners from 12 percent of the radio audience in the late 1990s to 22 percent in 2002. Since then, the numbers have remained about the same.

How to Find the Best Election Coverage

What can you do to make sure you're getting the best possible information from the media about the candidates and the issues at stake in the presidential race? The key, according to political experts, is to recognize the pluses and the minuses of the information you receive from all the different types of media. If you aren't getting enough information about the candidates and their positions on the issues from the mainstream press, check out some of the alternatives—for example, by surfing the Internet for more detailed breakdowns of where the candidates stand.

The key is to recognize the pluses and the minuses of the information you receive from all the different types of media.

And if the talk shows and the twenty-four-hour news networks aren't telling you how the candidates' ideas stand up to tougher scrutiny, keep an eye on the morning papers and the nightly news for some good old-fashioned political reporting.

Last but not least, if nobody seems to be covering the campaign and the issues to your satisfaction, be sure to speak up. Call or write your local newspaper or the local television or radio station and tell them you expect them to do a better job. Casting an informed vote can be tough, and the media have a responsibility to help you decide.

Beyond that, the Internet gives you unprecedented opportunities to express your views, questions, and general take on the world by starting your own blog. In May 2007, the blog search engine Technorati was tracking 71 million blogs, so you'll have plenty of company in the blogosphere. An alternative approach—and one

NETIZEN VOLUNTEERS: INVALUABLE AND UNPREDICTABLE

The democratic nature of the Internet—anyone can post—is precisely what makes its effects so hard to predict. Two examples from the current presidential campaign, both related to Democratic candidate Barack Obama, show how Internet action can present a candidate with unexpected benefits and unexpected problems.

In one case, a man reportedly acting independently created a video posted on YouTube that likened Hillary Clinton to Big Brother in 1984. It ended with the tagline BarackObama.com. The clever video, which used images from an anti-Microsoft ad that Apple Computer had sponsored years earlier, received millions of views and was in effect a great gift to the Obama campaign, as well as a blow to the Clinton cause.

In another case, a young volunteer built up a community on MySpace (myspace.com/barackobama) that eventually attracted 160,000 "friends" for the candidate. But in April 2007, when the volunteer and the official campaign had a falling out over whether the volunteer would be compensated, the messy controversy became a negative story that distracted from Obama's campaign.

In both instances, the fact that the volunteer was not a paid employee but a skilled and dedicated online activist—a "netizen"—made the volunteer impossible to control. Campaigns are learning that they must deal very carefully with expert free agents who can both help and hurt their candidates.

that may give your words greater visibility—is to contribute your thoughts to an existing, widely read blog.

Elections Go Online

The Internet came into its own as a resource for voters and political candidates during the 1996 presidential election. During the first presidential debate, Republican candidate Bob Dole included a plug for his Web site in his closing statement. In the hour after the debate, hundreds of thousands of Internet users visited the site, overloading the server and forcing the site to shut down.

Ever since then, people have been watching the Internet in all its varied forms—including candidate Web sites, e-mail, blogs, social networking sites like MySpace and video-sharing Web sites like YouTube—take on a growing role in presidential campaigns. It seems certain that the Internet will play a very significant role in the 2008 election, in ways that are difficult to predict beforehand.

More Americans than ever are getting news from the Internet, but it still lags behind some traditional media as a news source. According to a January 2007 Gallup poll, most Americans still get their daily news fix from their local TV station (55 percent) and their local newspaper (44 percent). Only 22 percent reported getting news daily from the Internet. That's up from 15 percent in 2000, but growth has slowed since 2004.

Still, with every election, the Internet has grown in importance. By 2007, nearly 70 percent of American adults were using the Internet, up from 61 percent in 2002 and a huge increase over the single digits of the mid-1990s. The fact that the medium has grown so quickly has meant that most political players have had to learn in stages how to use it effectively.

For candidates and campaign managers, the Internet's appeal as an election resource rests on the fact that it allows candidates and voters to be in contact without intermediaries. It has become a place to recruit volunteers and post press releases, speeches, biographical information, and position papers without having to filter everything through other media organizations.

The Internet has also become the cheapest, and therefore the most efficient, way to raise money for campaigns. People can respond to a call for donations on the Web without the campaign ever having to send them a mailer or pay for a mailing list. Parties and candidates tend to use their Web sites as highly efficient, inexpensive tools to maintain contact with supporters, rather than trying to contact Web surfers. Rallying the troops and getting them to show up at local events, to write letters to local newspapers, and to involve their friends are all effective ways to use the Internet.

The Howard Dean campaign of 2003–2004 got a big boost when some of its mostly young volunteers started using a social networking site called meetup.com to organize get-togethers called (naturally) meetups. The Dean campaign was soon the most popular group on meetup.com and found it had acquired both an unexpected buzz and thousands of new volunteers. To a large degree, it was done from the netroots up. That was new.

As 2008 approached, campaigns amped up their use of the Internet by plugging in to social networking Web sites, such as MySpace and Facebook, which had tens of millions of members. Because most members are in their teens and 20s, campaigns were being especially careful to maintain the right tone for their candidates' profiles: They must include some personal details to attract lots of "friends," but they don't want to appear phony. To capitalize on the new interest in politics, MySpace, by far the largest of the social sites, in 2007 set up a channel for candidates and campaign comments at http://impact.myspace.com.

To capitalize on the new interest in politics, MySpace, by far the largest of the social sites, in 2007 set up a channel for candidates and campaign comments.

As campaign professionals get better at using the Internet, they will almost certainly work on more effectively engaging the casual visitor to the candidate's own site, getting the person to subscribe to the site, and eventually become a volunteer and contributor.

Some experts believe that as Internet use continues to grow and more Americans are able to access election information from their homes, offices, and cars, we'll see an increase in political participation. The significant increase in youth voter turnout between the 2000 and the 2004 elections may be a sign that this is already starting to happen.

Whatever the case, there are numerous Web sites providing information about the 2008 presidential election, the candidates, and the issues. The following is just an introductory list, and many sites contain links to additional resources.

WEB SITE DIRECTORY

- VOTE411.org The League of Women Voters' nonpartisan resource for election and voting information. Through VOTE411, citizens can find such items as voter registration and absentee ballot rules, early voting provisions, ID requirements, candidate information, a national polling place locator and much more. www.VOTE411.org.

- C-SPAN's 2008 Vote Web page. Offers video of candidate speeches and campaign events and links to candidate Web sites: www.c-span.org; click on "American Politics/ Road to the White House."

- Factcheck.org. Nonpartisan site checks the accuracy of political ads and allegations. Sponsored by the Annenberg Public Policy Center at the University of Pennsylvania: www.factcheck.org.

- Federal Election Commission. Official site of the government agency that regulates campaign finance. Information on campaign contributions to candidates, but you may have to do some digging. Worth checking out—the "Press Office" section: www.fec.gov.

- Grolier Presents the American Presidency. Offers age-appropriate information for children and youth on the presidency, the Electoral College, and presidential history: ap.grolier.com.

- League of Women Voters. Provides a wealth of nonpartisan policy information useful for casting an informed vote during election season. Also included are links to state and local sites and information about voter registration: www.lwv.org.

- MySpace Impact. The huge social networking site where you can not only find out about a candidate, you can sign up to be their "friend:" http://impact.myspace.com.

- PollingReport.com. Nonpartisan site offers updated and archived public opinion polling on elections and public policy: www.pollingreport.com.

- Democratic National Committee. Official party site offers critical views of Republican candidates and positions, as well as information on the convention and party platform, party rules: www.democrats.org.

- Republican National Committee. Official party site offers GOP views on issues and Democratic candidates, the upcoming convention and party platform, party rules: www.rnc.org.

CHAPTER 5

Money: Who Gives It, Who Gets It

"Money is the mother's milk of politics," said the legendary California politician Jess Unruh, and when it comes to electing a president, he was certainly right. The conventional wisdom is that a credible candidate for president in 2008 will have to obtain at least $50 million dollars to pay for television advertising, travel, campaign staff, consultants, and other campaign costs. And that's just for the primaries.

Overall, 2008 is likely to see the first $1 billion election, with the major party nominees for president each having spent over $500 million by the time Americans go to the polls in November. After adding the tens of millions of dollars that will be spent by all other challengers, the total cost of the 2008 presidential race may reach $1.4 billion, almost twice the $760 million spent by all candidates in 2004.

Concerns about fund-raising techniques, combined with the astounding amount of money being raised and spent, has prompted many Americans to wonder if this is a good way to choose a president. Reform advocates in particular are concerned that only candidates who can raise many millions of dollars can mount a serious campaign. This obstacle means that—unless they are personally very

A credible candidate for president in 2008 will have to obtain at least $50 million dollars to pay for campaign costs.

rich—candidates must tailor their approaches to appeal to moneyed interests.

THE COST OF RUNNING FOR PRESIDENT

These are the total amounts of money raised in 2003–2004 by the five best-funded presidential candidates in the 2004 general election, according to the Center for Responsive Politics. Totals include federal matching funds.

Note: Both the Bush campaign and Kerry campaigns declined to accept federal funds in the primary elections, but did take federal funds for the general election.

Candidate	Total Funds Raised (in millions $)	Federal Funds (in millions $)
George W. Bush (Republican)	$367.2	$74.6
John Kerry (Democratic)	$328.5	$74.6
Ralph Nader (Reform, Populist, Independent)	$4.6	$.8
Michael Badnarik (Libertarian)	$1.1	$0
Michael Peroutka (Constitution)	$.7	$0

ATTACKS OF THE PACs

Groups that want to have influence in U.S. politics often form political action committees. PACs can contribute to candidates and parties and can spend money independently, such as by running their own ads.

Business corporations and labor unions are prohibited from donating to candidates or spending their own money on campaigns, but they can legally form PACS funded by donations from their individual members.

These are the twenty PACs that spent the most money during the last election cycle, 2003–2004, according to the Federal Election Commission. In most cases, only a small fraction of the money listed was spent on presidential campaigns.

America Coming Together (Democratic)   *$33.7 million*

MoveOn PAC   *$31.8 million*
(liberal Democrats)

EMILY's List   *$27.5 million*
(Democratic, pro-abortion rights)

Service Employees   *$14.7 million*
International Union

AFSCME   *$13.9 million*
(public employees union)

National Rifle Association   *$12.8 million*

United Auto Workers   *$10.8 million*

DRIVE (Teamsters Union)	$10.7 million
Republican Issues Campaign	$7.7 million
National Association of Realtors	$7.7 million
American Federation of Teachers	$7.3 million
New York State Teachers (union)	$6.9 million
1199 Service Employees International Union	$6.8 million
Communications Workers of America	$6.7 million
International Brotherhood of Electrical Workers (union)	$6.5 million
Association of Trial Lawyers of America	$6.4 million
Pro-Life Campaign Committee	$5.8 million
21st Century Democrats	$5.5 million
United Food & Commercial Workers	$5.4 million
Freshmen PAC (Republican congressional)	$5.0 million

In 2004, when the primary and general elections were all over, the Bush campaign had received more than $367 million, and the Kerry campaign more than $328 million—both hefty increases over 2000. In addition, the Democratic National Committee spent about $120 million to support their presidential candidate, and the Republicans probably spent about the same, though these payments were not officially part of the candidates' campaigns.

The Center for Responsive Politics, a nonpartisan think tank in Washington, estimated that at least $1.2 billion was spent by all players in the 2004 presidential race (see table on page 72), but they acknowledge that their estimate is probably much too low. The truth is that in recent presidential elections, so many big-spending groups have been throwing so much money around in so many ways that it is impossible for even the experts to keep track of total spending.

THE COST OF CONSULTANTS

According to a 2006 study by the Center for Public Integrity, a Washington, D.C., investigative group, the cost of presidential campaigns is pushed up in part by consultants—these are private firms hired by the campaign organizations to supply expert advice. By far the most expensive of these are the media consultants, who develop strategies, get the TV and radio ads made, and then place the ads. Interestingly, these media consultants take a commission on all media buys, so they have an incentive to spend as much as possible.

In the 2004 campaign, the Bush campaign spent over $235 million on consultants—well over half its total expenditures. Of that, a hefty $177 million was spent through one company, Maverick Media, the campaign's principal media consultant. On the Democratic side, the story is similar. The Kerry campaign spent $163 million on consultants, including $132 million on its main media consultant, Riverfront Media.

WHERE THE MONEY COMES FROM

The Center for Responsive Politics put together this rough breakdown of spending for the 2004 presidential race. These are figures for all candidates, both Democratic and Republican, in both the primaries and the general election. The Center, which sponsors the excellent Web site www.opensecrets.org, acknowledges that its subtotals and its grand total are almost certainly underestimates.

Individual contributions to presidential candidates	$617 million
Public funds to presidential candidates and party conventions	$207 million
527 group spending*	$187 million
Convention host committee spending	$139 million
Democratic and Republican National Committees	$92 million
PAC contributions to presidential candidates	$4 million
Candidate self-financing	$556,000
TOTAL	**$1.2 billion**

* This is a conservative figure that includes projected spending only by the following 527 groups: America, Coming Together, Media Fund, MoveOn.org, Progress for America and Swift Boat Veterans for Truth (now called Swift Vets and POWs for Truth).

After many attempts, Congress in 2002 passed a law to try to plug some of the loopholes in the campaign finance regulatory system. As we discuss various aspects of campaign financing in this chapter, we'll look at the Bipartisan Campaign Reform Act of 2002—also known as the McCain-Feingold Act, after its chief sponsors, Senator John McCain (R-Ariz.) and Senator Russ Feingold (D-Wis.)—and how it is affecting the getting and spending of campaign cash.

Why They Donate: The Quest for Influence

Why do so many people and interest groups put so much money into presidential campaigns and other political campaigns? Many, especially large, organized donors, contribute because they have certain things they want the government to do (or not do), and they are convinced that spending money will increase their influence.

Sometimes the interests are economic—maybe the hospital industry wants health care rules that will increase payments to hospitals. Or the interests may be ideological—both the pro-choice and anti-abortion lobbies spend many millions to increase the chances that the president and members of Congress will listen to them.

Small donors give for a variety of reasons—ideological agreement with a candidate, anger over some public matter, or just to be part of the action. In some wealthy communities and social circles, people host candidate fund-raisers to meet the candidates or to boost their social standing.

Because money is so essential to the political process, trying to limit the influence of moneyed interests in U.S. politics is extremely difficult. When laws are passed restricting contributions, special interests are often very resourceful in finding new ways to raise and spend funds. A prime example of skillful circumvention of the law has taken place in recent years, as funders and political groups have adapted to the Bipartisan Campaign Reform Act of 2002. When donors were prohibited from giving soft money directly to the political parties, they were able to achieve some of their goals by creating or donating to freestanding political groups like 527s and 501(c)s (see section on "Groups That Influence Elections," page 41). Despite the resourcefulness of moneyed interests in finding ways to influence the political process, most observers believe that the ongoing

effort to "clean up" U.S. politics has had major beneficial effects —
both in curbing the worst spending excesses and exposing to public
scrutiny the flow of funds.

BUNDLING: PUTTING MONEY TOGETHER

"Bundling" contributions is another way companies and interest
groups can bypass legal limits on campaign contributions. Bundling means pooling a number of smaller contributions together
in one package, in order to maximize the political influence of
the bundler.

For example, the widget industry's PAC can legally donate only
$5,000 to a candidate in any election cycle. But this same PAC
(or any widget executive) can solicit hundreds of contributions
from individuals in the industry. If it wants to, it can hand the
entire bundle of contributions to the campaign at one time, creating a sizeable impact on behalf of the widget industry.

Under BCRA—aka the McCain-Feingold Act—the maximum
individual contribution has been raised from $1,000 to $2,000
(now adjusted for inflation to $2,300) which makes bundling
more lucrative than ever.

The 2000 campaign of George W. Bush raised bundling to a new,
higher level. His campaign recognized supporters as "Pioneers"
when they had raised $100,000 in donations. In 2004, the Bush
campaign added new categories—Rangers and Super-Rangers
—for people who raised $200,000 or $300,000.

Not wanting to be left behind, the Kerry campaign in 2004 recognized their super-bundlers as "Patriots" ($100,000)
and "Trustees" ($250,000).

Bundling is not entirely new, but it is a growth industry.
EMILY's List, a pro-Democratic, pro-abortion-rights PAC,
has been successful at bundling for many years. So has
the Club for Growth, a pro-business Republican PAC.

On occasion, employers pressure employees into making contributions to candidates or committees favored by the business's top executives. In fact, in 2006 the Federal Election Commission levied its biggest fine ever—$3.8 million—on the mortgage company Freddie Mac. One of the company's offenses was using corporate staff and resources to solicit campaign donations from the corporation's employees.

Sometimes bundling is done without a formal conduit that groups the contributions. So, for example, many executives from a given company or industry can send contributions to a certain campaign in a short time. Even though the contributions are not delivered in the same envelope, the donors can make it clear that these are not isolated contributions, but part of an organized effort, for example by marking their checks in a special way.

In 2007, campaign reform advocates were pushing for new rules that would require lobbyists and other bundlers to disclose their activities to public scrutiny.

Watergate: The Wake-Up Call

The effect of campaign contributions on politics has been a concern throughout America's history. Congress passed a law making corporate contributions to federal campaigns illegal in 1907. But the issue received more public attention in the 1970s, when the Watergate scandal convinced citizens and lawmakers alike that something needed to be done to stem the flow of special-interest money to politicians and their campaigns.

The introduction of television advertising as a campaign tool in the 1950s and 1960s dramatically increased the cost of campaigning for public office, and the ensuing scramble for funds left many concerned that American democracy was being harmed. Disclosures during the Watergate investigations that corporations and

The Watergate scandal convinced citizens and lawmakers alike that something needed to be done to stem the flow of special-interest money to politicians and their campaigns.

wealthy individuals had made illegal and "laundered" cash contributions to President Richard Nixon's reelection campaign only confirmed people's worst suspicions.

Reform's First Steps

Before the Watergate scandal, President Richard Nixon had signed into law the Federal Election Campaign Act (FECA) of 1971. Among other things, the law required candidates and donors to report their political contributions and spending.

After the Watergate scandal of 1972–1974, which involved big donors to President Nixon's campaign, legislators revisited the campaign finance issue. The FECA amendments signed into law in 1974 represented the most comprehensive campaign finance legislation ever adopted at the federal level. Among other things, the law:

- Strengthened requirements for reporting of campaign contributions and spending
- Set new limits on spending in congressional elections
- Limited the size of contributions to candidates and parties and put a cap on an individual's total contributions per campaign cycle
- Created a system of public financing to support the campaigns of presidential candidates who agree to specific contribution and spending limits
- Created an independent agency, the Federal Election Commission, to enforce the new rules

More than thirty years later, most of these basic principles—disclosure of finances, limits on amounts and sources of contributions, and public funds for presidential candidates who agree to play by the rules—still govern campaign finance in America. But there have been a number of changes along the way.

The Court Weighs In

In 1976, the Supreme Court held parts of the FECA unconstitutional with its decision in Buckley v. Valeo. The Court declared that mandatory spending limits on congressional campaigns violated the Constitution's free-speech protections. However, the justices let stand the spending limits for presidential candidates who accepted public funds, asserting that these were voluntary limits and thus could pass constitutional muster.

The Court also ruled in Buckley that independent groups and individuals could spend unlimited amounts of money—a decision that has had an enormous and lasting impact. Though the Court may have been thinking of small, local groups, this decision gave rise to large amounts of money being spent by national interest groups.

Later in the 1970s, Congress made additional changes in the law. It required reporting of "independent expenditures" by special interests in support of candidates' campaigns. It allowed the political parties to spend limited amounts of money in coordination with their candidates' campaigns in the general election. And it allowed the political parties to receive unlimited amounts of money to be spent on "party-building" activities, such as voter-registration drives.

This last provision, along with decisions by the Federal Election Commission, created the "soft-money" loophole. This loophole was used—up through the 2002 elections—to channel hundreds of millions of dollars from the political parties to their candidates' campaigns. The reason soft money (money not subject to federal limits) is seen as a problem is that it allows wealthy individuals and groups to bypass the limits on contributions in campaign finance law. (Later in this chapter we discuss hard and soft money in some detail.) State and local parties were never controlled by federal law, and they soon realized that they could accept unrestricted soft money and spend it independently on federal elections.

Public Funding of Presidential Elections: How It Works

Candidates in every presidential election since 1976 have been eligible to receive public funds to cover some of the costs of their campaigns. The idea behind public funding of presidential elections is to make candidates less dependent on contributions from special interests and wealthy donors. Public money for presidential elections comes from a fund supported by the "taxpayer check-off" on individual tax returns. These rules have stayed basically the same since 1976, though the amounts of money involved have been

FOR CONGRESS, NO SPENDING LIMITS

Because of the Supreme Court's decision in 1976 that mandatory spending limits on political campaigns are unconstitutional, there is no ceiling on what a candidate can spend on a race for Congress. In the presidential election, by contrast, the spending limits on the candidates are considered voluntary and apply only if the candidate agrees to accept public funds.

The spending for House and Senate races has risen at a steady and fast pace. An all-time record was set in 2000, when New Jersey investment banker Jon Corzine ran for the U.S. Senate. Though he had never held public office, he beat a former governor in the Democratic primary and a U.S. representative in the general election. The cost to Corzine: an estimated $60 million in personal funds—about twice what anyone had ever spent before to win a Senate seat.

generally indexed to inflation. For example, the ceiling on each candidate's spending in the primary election period was about $13 million in 1976; in 2004, it was about $50 million.

Primary Matching Funds

During the primaries, candidates can receive partial public funding in the form of matching payments, with the federal government matching all contributions up to $250. In other words, if you give $500 to a candidate during the primaries, the federal government will chip in its maximum of $250, but only if the candidate meets certain criteria. These are:

+ The candidate must show broad-based public support by receiving at least $5,000 in contributions of $250 or less in twenty or more states.
+ The candidate must agree to a national limit on campaign spending for all primary elections.

+ The candidate must agree to spending limits established for each state based on its voting-age population.
+ The candidate cannot spend more than $50,000 of his or her own funds on the campaign.

Before 2004, few major-party candidates chose to forgo public financing in the primaries. The first successful nominee to do so was George W. Bush in 2000.

In 2004, however, three serious candidates went outside the public financing system: President George W. Bush, and Democrats Howard Dean and John Kerry.

After the primaries, the national political parties also receive some public financing to help pay for their nominating conventions. In 2004, each party received $14.9 million for that purpose.

General Election Funding

In addition to the primary matching funds, the presidential nominees of the major parties become eligible for public funding to support all campaign costs associated with the general election in the fall. In order to receive the general election funds, a candidate must limit spending to the amount he or she receives from the federal

HOW MUCH CAN YOU GIVE A CANDIDATE?

Want to support a candidate yourself? Individuals may contribute up to $2,300 to a presidential candidate during the primary election campaign, whether or not the candidate accepts public matching funds.

During the general election, major-party candidates who have accepted public funding may not accept individual campaign contributions, with minor exceptions. However, if a candidate does not accept public financing for the general election (and some experts think that might happen for the first time in 2008), then individuals can contribute another $2,300 to a presidential candidate for the general election.

THE SELF-FUNDED CAMPAIGN

The sky's the limit when a presidential candidate refuses to accept public funds and the accompanying restrictions on campaign contributions and spending. In the 1990s, two candidates said no to public funds while digging into their personal fortunes to cover the costs of their campaigns.

The first was Ross Perot, who in 1992 spent $60 million of his own money on the race, most of it to pay for television time. In 1996, by contrast, Perot decided to accept public matching funds and, as a result, could spend just $50,000 of his own money. Steve Forbes, another wealthy businessman, spent $37 million on his unsuccessful bid to capture the Republican nomination in 1996 and another $32 million in 2000, but never ignited broad public enthusiasm.

Saying no to public financing means that a candidate misses out on up to $18 million in federal matching funds in the primary season (though most candidates receive far less). And if the candidate passes on public funding for the general election, that would mean missing out on an estimated $85 million dollars in 2008.

government, while pledging not to accept private contributions for the campaign. In 2004, the two major-party nominees were eligible for general election funding of $74.6 million apiece. That figure rises to $85 million in 2008.

What About Third-Party Candidates?

Third-party candidates also are eligible for public funding to support their general election campaigns, provided the party's nominee received between 5 and 25 percent of the popular vote in the previous presidential election. (If a party receives more than 25 percent, it is considered a major party and becomes subject to the same rules as the Democratic and Republican parties.)

If a third party did not field a candidate last time but is doing so in the current election, its candidate may receive significant public funding for that election after the campaign is over if he or she receives 5 percent or more of the vote. In addition, minor-party candidates can receive much smaller amounts in matching funds if they show they are running a serious campaign, say, by appearing on the ballot in a number of states.

Third-party candidate Ross Perot received about $29 million in public funding to support his 1996 campaign on the Reform Party line. The amount of public funds made available to Perot was based on his impressive finish in the 1992 election, when he attracted 19 percent of the popular vote.

For the 2000 race, the Reform Party nominated Pat Buchanan, who received $12.6 million in public funds, based on Perot's performance in 1996. (Buchanan himself got less than 1 percent of the popular vote.)

No party other than the Republicans and Democrats will receive campaign money in 2008.

In the 2004 presidential election, no third-party candidate received 5 percent of the vote, so no party other than the Republicans and Democrats will receive campaign money in 2008—at least not until the election is over.

Getting around the Rules: Hard and Soft Money

Beginning in the late 1970s and continuing until 2002, federal election laws and FEC rulings created a system in which there were two types of funds available for campaigns and political parties. Those were known as hard money and soft money.

(Soft money has become a smaller concern since 2002 because of the reform law BCRA.)

Hard money is money raised according to strict federal rules, which limit the amount per contribution (now at $2,300 per candidate) and the total amounts that an individual or group may contribute to candidates and parties during any given election cycle. Hard money cannot come from corporations or unions. Donations of more than two hundred dollars must be disclosed to the Federal Election Commission and are public record. But once you've raised this hard money, you can spend it on any campaign activity—paying

KEEPING DOWN THE COST OF RUNNING FOR PRESIDENT

The average cost of running for the U.S. House of Representatives grew enormously between 1976 and 2000—from $73,000 to $683,000. That's an increase of 832 percent. But during those same twenty-four years, the cost of running for president (for candidates who accepted public funding) went from about $35 million to $113 million—an increase of just 222 percent. In fact, it just kept up with the rate of inflation.

The contrast between these two rates of increase is strong evidence that the presidential campaign finance system accomplished an important goal—it kept down the cost of running for president. (It must be acknowledged that there was a massive inflow of soft money into presidential campaigns during this period—so the claim of success is qualified.)

The public financing system for presidential campaigns began to break down in 2004, and there's a real possibility that neither major party candidate will accept public funds in 2008. The League of Women Voters and other clean-government advocates are working with congressional allies to revitalize the system for 2012.

campaign staff, buying bumper stickers, buying TV advertising, whatever.

Under federal law, soft money (funds not subject to federal law) was much more loosely regulated. The hard-money rules limiting amounts and sources of contributions did not apply. For many years, soft money could be raised in unlimited amounts, from any source, including corporations and unions, subject only to state law. Until the campaign finance law of 2002, it was common for the national political party committees to receive six-figure donations of soft money. Donors included major corporations, unions, individuals, trade associations, and other interest groups.

In the 1990s, soft money donations grew enormously—from $86 million in 1992 to $495 million in 2000. Many in Congress came to see this flood of unregulated cash as a serious problem that was defeating the goals of modern campaign finance law.

BCRA, the McCain-Feingold Act, contained language that aimed to solve the soft money problem. It prohibits the national party committees from receiving soft money at all. Instead, the parties must rely on hard money—contributions of no more than $57,000 every two years from any individual—rather than unlimited amounts from any source.

BCRA was an important reform in cleaning up the finances of the national parties. But did it abolish "soft money" from American politics? In a strict sense it did: the national party committees are no longer receiving those six-figure contributions. Other observers would say that in a broader sense soft money still plays a role in campaigns in

THE McCAIN-FEINGOLD ACT (BCRA) OF 2002

Throughout the 1990s, campaign reform forces tried again and again to get a stronger law passed by Congress. Leading the charge in the Senate were Senators John McCain, R-Ariz., and Russell Feingold, D-Wis., with Representatives Chris Shays, R-Conn., and Marty Meehan, D-Mass., providing the leadership in the House of Representatives. The major goals of the McCain-Feingold bill were to curb the growing influence of unlimited soft-money contributions to the Democratic and Republican national party organizations and to limit big-dollar special-interest funding for campaign advertising.

In March 2002, Congress finally passed a version of McCain-Feingold, officially called the Bipartisan Campaign Reform Act. President George W. Bush signed it, and it went into effect the day after the November 5, 2002, election.

KEY PROVISIONS OF BCRA:
  · National party organizations are forbidden to accept
    soft money contributions. They may only accept hard
    money—contributions subject to federal limits on who
    may donate and how much.

- Hard-money limits are increased. For example, the amount an individual may donate to a campaign went from $1,000 per election to $2,000 in 2004 and (adjusted for inflation) $2,300 in 2008.
- Corporations, unions, and trade associations were prohibited from financing "electioneering communications" within sixty days of a general election and thirty days of a primary election. An electioneering communication is one that refers to a federal candidate and is targeted toward that person's state or district. However, as we explain later in this chapter, this section of BCRA is no longer fully in effect because of a 2007 Supreme Court decision.

As soon as the law was signed, more than eighty plaintiffs, including both major political parties, filed suit in federal court to stop BCRA from going into effect. Those lawsuits were consolidated into one major case, McConnell v. FEC. In December 2003, the Supreme Court, to the surprise of many observers, upheld virtually the entire McCain-Feingold Act. Consequently, the elections of 2004 and 2006 were held under the new law.

Overall, reform advocates think that BCRA has been successful in stopping the flow of soft money to the Democratic and Republican parties. Though critics warned that BCRA would damage the parties, the two parties have raised just as much money after BCRA as before. But instead of getting that money in six-figure soft-money donations, they're raising it in small hard-money donations and have added more than a million small donors to their rolls.

McCain-Feingold was also successful in curbing questionable advocacy ads in 2004 and 2006, though that will be less true in 2008.

other ways — through big donations to state party committees, party conventions, presidential inaugurations, 527s and other channels.

Evading the Soft-Money Ban

As soon as BCRA passed, the national parties and political operators began working out ways they could adapt to the law and continue getting funds from their biggest contributors. One significant exception to BCRA is that state and local parties can still receive

TOP 527 ORGANIZATIONS IN 2004

527s gained new prominence in the 2004 election and were an important conduit for major contributions not regulated by federal campaign finance law. Some extremely wealthy Americans gave millions to 527s to influence the presidential election. These are the 527s that received the most in donations in 2003 and 2004. Only some of the funds listed below went for presidential campaigns.

Victory Campaign 2004 (Democratic)	*$71.8 million*
America Coming Together (Democratic)	*$54.3 million*
SEIU Political Education and Action Local Fund (union)	*$46.1 million*
Progress for America Voter Fund (Republican)	*$44.9 million*
Republican Governors Association	*$33.8 million*
Democratic Governors Association	*$24.2 million*
AFSCME Special Account (union)	*$22.2 million*
Swift Boat Veterans for Truth (anti-Kerry, Republican)	*$17.0 million*
Media Fund (Democratic)	*$15.0 million*
College Republican National Committee	*$12.8 million*

New Democrat Network—Non-Federal	*$12.7 million*
MoveOn.org Voter Fund (liberal Democratic)	*$12.6 million*
Citizens for a Strong Senate (Democratic)	*$10.9 million*
Republican State Leadership Committee	*$10.8 million*
Sierra Club Voter Education Fund	*$8.7 million*
Club for Growth (conservative Republican)	*$8.2 million*
1199 SEIU Non-Federal Committee (union)	*$8.1 million*
EMILY'S List (Democratic, pro-abortion-rights)	*$7.7 million*
Voices For Working Families (Democratic)	*$7.5 million*
IBEW Educational Committee (union)	*$6.7 million*

Source: Center for Public Integrity

soft money, as long as it's not spent on federal campaigns. (State laws may regulate soft money, though.)

An important loophole, which became very significant, was the use of "527 organizations" named for the section of the Internal Revenue Code that covers them. These groups are unlike PACs in that they are not regulated by the Federal Election Commission. More importantly, they can accept "soft money" (using that term broadly) in unlimited amounts—and they did that to an amazing degree in 2004. (They get away with this because they supposedly engage only in issue advocacy and not in campaigning for candidates—though in practice it can be hard to tell the difference.) Much of the 527 activity in 2004 was funded through very large donations. An estimated 80 percent came from individuals who contributed $250,000 or more. The overall contributions to Democratic-leaning 527s came to $265 million, considerably more than the $154 million raised by Republican-leaning 527s. Some of the donations to the Democratic side came from extremely wealthy liberal business execs like mega-investor George Soros and insurance company chair Peter Lewis, each of whom gave about $23 million to America Coming Together.

The best known 527 of the 2004 campaign was Swift Boat Veterans for Truth, which attacked the Vietnam war record of Democratic candidate John Kerry and generated a lot of free media coverage as well.

Other large donors found ways to use another type of nonprofit organization to have an impact on political campaigns—these are known as 501(c) organizations, for the section of the tax code that governs them. 501(c)s are even less strictly regulated than 527s. While most of these are nonpolitical, charitable, educational, or similar organizations, some played an important role in the 2004 campaign.

As if that weren't enough, corporations and interest groups have also found that despite the soft money ban, they can make large donations to the parties toward their national conventions and inaugurations. (Thanks to lax interpretations by the Federal Election Commission, these are not considered donations to the parties.) As a result, corporations and other interest groups were permitted to give at least $103 million to the two big party conventions and at least $17 million to the second Bush inauguration of January 2005.

Independent Advocacy: Really Independent?

For interest groups that want to influence elections, help favored candidates, and damage candidates they don't like, there are ways to do so independently of the official campaigns and political parties.

Independent Expenditures

Individuals and political action committees can spend unlimited amounts of money on advertising and other activities endorsing individual candidates. This is perfectly legal as long as the spending is disclosed to the FEC and is not coordinated with a candidate's campaign. (The reason for this rule is that "independent" activities that are coordinated with the campaign are not truly independent. They are awfully close to being just another activity of the campaign, and under the law should be regulated as part of the campaign.)

Political parties can also spend hard (federally regulated) money independently in support of candidates. Under BCRA, a party has to make a choice at the time a candidate is nominated. It may choose to make independent expenditures in support of its candidate. In this case, the amount it can spend is unlimited, but the money must be spent without consulting with the candidate. Or it can spend a limited amount while coordinating its spending with the candidate.

Campaign managers are often wary of genuinely independent spenders because their activities may or may not be in sync with the main campaign strategy. Still, many organizations thrive on raising funds to support or oppose candidates, and the independent expenditure rules are well suited to their purposes.

Issue Advocacy

This is advertising designed to build support for a candidate without explicitly telling the audience to vote for the candidate. The problem here is that issue advocacy commercials allow special interest groups to escape the source limitations and reporting requirements they have to abide by when making political contributions or independent expenditures on a candidate's behalf. This has made issue advocacy an increasingly popular way for corporations, labor unions, and others to try to influence the outcome of federal elections while avoiding detection (see chapter 3 for more on special interests).

Under BCRA, such issue ads were still allowed, though special restrictions were placed on TV and radio advertising sponsored by corporations (including nonprofit corporations) and labor unions. Those groups were prohibited from sponsoring "electioneering" ads in a candidate's district in the sixty days before a general election or the thirty days before a primary. This meant no ads mentioning any candidates.

However, in June 2007, the U.S. Supreme Court reduced in scope the impact of this BCRA prohibition. In the case of Federal Election Commission v. Wisconsin Right to Life, the Court said that some "issue ads" that mention candidates in the key period right before elections may not be prohibited by BCRA, because those ads are free speech protected by the First Amendment.

Advocates of clean elections were disappointed by the Supreme Court ruling, which appeared to re-open the door to a flood of corporate- and union-sponsored advertising that would have the practical effect of supporting candidates. What's more, these advocates were concerned that the FEC would interpret the Supreme Court decision to allow most advertising of this type.

Another worry: the Supreme Court, having weakened the BCRA rule on issue advertising, might soon overturn it completely. Because of changes in its membership, the Court had become more conservative between 2003, when it upheld almost all of BCRA, and 2007, when it decided to reverse its decision of four years earlier and chip away at the law.

As this book was written in 2007, political players and observers of all stripes were anxious to learn how the new Supreme Court ruling would work out in practice as the 2008 election season approached.

Funding Presidential Campaigns: A System In Trouble

The system of funding presidential campaigns worked pretty well from its start in 1976 into the 1990s. It helped keep the candidates' pursuit of money at least somewhat under control and has been efficiently and cleanly run (see the box "Keeping Down the Cost of Running for President," page 82).

The public financing system is voluntary for candidates—it offers them a deal, which must be made attractive for them to agree to it. The deal is: If you agree to limit the amount of money you raise and spend and play by our rules, we will give you lots of money for your campaign—partial funding in the primaries and full funding in the general election. Up until 2000, almost all candidates found this set of trade-offs agreeable and participated.

In 2000, the system began to show weakness, when George W. Bush declined to accept public financing for the primaries and instead raised more money from private sources. Both he and his Democratic opponent accepted public financing in the general election, though.

In 2004, both President Bush and Democrat John Kerry turned down public financing for the primaries. Instead, Bush raised $270 million in private funds and Kerry raised $235 million—far more than they would have received under public financing. While both candidates accepted public funding for the general election, it was clear that the system was in big trouble.

In 2008, it seems very likely that the most serious candidates (that is, the best financed) will forgo public financing in both the primary and general elections.

In 2008, it seems very likely that the most serious candidates (that is, the best financed) will forgo public financing in both the primary and general elections. Senator Hillary Rodham Clinton said early on that she would pass up public financing, which tended to make it difficult for other candidates to stay on the tighter public funding budget.

Clean-government advocates were deeply concerned that the entire structure of public financing of presidential elections might come crashing down in 2008.

To forestall that possibility, the League of Women Voters and seven other clean-government organizations in March 2007 publicly called on all Democratic and Republican candidates to pledge to use public funds for the general election and to fix the system.

Serious Problems, Possible Solutions

Here are some of the key problems that experts see in the current system, and some possible solutions:

- The public funding offered to the candidates is insufficient. Simple solution: Increase substantially the public funds grant to participating candidates.

• The spending limits candidates must accept in order to receive public funds are too low. One suggestion: if a candidate who has accepted public funding faces an opponent who is spending a great deal more, the public funds grant to the participating candidate could be instantly doubled or more.

• The nomination schedule has become extremely "front-loaded"—that is, the serious action takes place very early (see chapter 7). So the parties' nominees may be effectively chosen by mid-February, but the financing system has not adapted. It still makes payments starting with January 1 of election year, and monthly after that. That's too late. One possible remedy, proposed by some members of Congress, is to move the starting date for payment to July 1 of the previous year.

Presidential campaign funding depends on a voluntary check-off on individuals' federal tax returns, which does not cost the taxpayer anything.

• The system is running short of money. Presidential campaign funding depends on a voluntary check-off on individuals' federal tax returns, which does not cost the taxpayer anything. But for reasons unknown, the percentage of taxpayers who check this box has dropped steadily, from 29 percent in 1981 to 10 percent in 2006. Possible remedies include increasing the maximum

HOW TO REFORM CAMPAIGN FINANCE: TWO PROPOSALS

With the public financing system in serious trouble, the idea of undertaking a comprehensive reform—coming up with a brand new plan—starts to look interesting. One potential benefit of comprehensive reform: It might make it possible for a person to run a credible presidential campaign without appealing to large numbers of wealthy donors. This could open the political dialogue to more varied voices.

Here are two suggested measures that proponents say could drastically improve the campaign finance picture.

- The clean elections option. Candidates could qualify for public funding in the primaries by getting a large number of very small contributions—say five dollars. From this point on, they would not raise or receive any private contributions at all, thereby freeing them from the money chase. This would in effect make the primary campaign similar to the general election campaign, where presidential candidates can get full public funding. This idea has been in effect for several years in Maine and Arizona, and since 2005 in Connecticut. In these states it is used by most eligible candidates. New Jersey, New Mexico, North Carolina and Vermont, as well as some local jurisdictions, have also adopted the concept.
- Free air time for candidates. Purchasing advertising on TV consumes a large chunk of campaign budgets. As Democratic candidate Bill Bradley quipped in 2000, "You simply transfer money from contributors to television stations." TV stations (and to a lesser degree radio stations) make scads of money from campaign ads. In fact, many stations raise their rates for political ads as Election Day approaches. This increases the amounts candidates must raise, making the quest for donations more urgent.

One way to improve this situation would be to require TV and radio stations to offer free airtime to candidates. This could include airtime for candidate forums, debates, and interviews and providing qualified candidates with vouchers for free ads in the weeks before an election.

PART II

THE PROCESS

CHAPTER 6

Early Action

Legend has it that Lamar Alexander, the former Tennessee governor who ran for the Republican nomination for president in 1996 and lost, wasted no time kicking off his 2000 presidential bid. According to the Washington Post, the day after Bob Dole lost to Bill Clinton in the November 1996 election, Alexander was on the phone raising money for his next run.

Presidential campaigns have always started well in advance of the first caucus or party primary. The 2008 election has followed, and even accelerated, this pattern. Because of the front-loaded primary schedule and the need to raise increasing amounts of campaign cash, contenders in the 2008 presidential contest were busy campaigning and raising money in 2006.

Contenders in the 2008 presidential contest were busy campaigning and raising money in 2006.

Some experts on politics used to call this competition for funds "the invisible primary"—but it's not invisible any more. In fact, the candidates' fundraising totals for the first quarter of 2007 got lots of news coverage, because those numbers were seen as an early indicator of how well their campaigns were doing. For the 2008 election, it would be more accurate to just call this competition "the money primary."

According to one theory, whoever has raised the most money in the year before the election will win the nomination. That may usually be true, but in 2003 Howard Dean was an exception to that rule: He was the top Democratic fundraiser at the end of the year, but lost the nomination. Nonetheless, approaching the 2008 election, with several strong candidates running for president in both the Republican and Democratic parties, it seemed certain that the money primary would be vigorously contested.

Laying the Groundwork: Campaigning Unannounced

A presidential campaign begins long before a contender's formal announcement of candidacy. In the earliest stages of the campaign, "unannounced" presidential candidates try to build a favorable image in their party and throughout the country by making frequent public speeches and appearing at important party functions. It is now common for presidential candidates to start visiting lead-off primary and caucus states such as Iowa and New Hampshire two years or more before voters in those states choose among their parties' contenders. The goals of these early visits are to build name recognition, make important connections with party leaders, and create a foundation of support in states that traditionally have set the tone for the primary season.

Sometimes those early contacts involve more than speeches and handshakes. Candidates often distribute donations to party organizations or local campaigns in key states like Iowa and New Hampshire as a way to build name recognition and goodwill.

The Money Chase, Part I: PAC It Up

Another established practice among would-be candidates long before a presidential election is to establish one or more political action committees. These "leadership PACs" allow candidates to collect contributions that do not count against their presidential fundraising and spending limits—as long as they haven't officially filed with the Federal Election Commission as candidates for president.

One trick that many presidential candidates now employ in their early fund-raising is to create leadership PACs in states with lax election laws. Unlike PACs established under federal election rules, which are restricted to collecting individual contributions of $5,000 or less, these state-level PACs can collect contributions of any amount and from any source, subject only to state law.

GOP candidate Mitt Romney, for example, set up a PAC in Alabama without donor limits. It collected a donation of $86,000 from a Colorado businessman—far more than the $5,000 per year that can legally be given to a federally registered PAC.

Politicians often use their PAC funds to help build support for their candidacies. Senator John McCain, for example, doled out more than $2 million from his leadership PAC to Republican candidates and conservative causes in 2005 and 2006. And Senator Barack Obama spent over $700,000 to support Democrats in more than forty states, focusing on three states that hold early primaries or caucuses: Iowa, New Hampshire, and Nevada.

The ostensible purpose of the PACs is to make contributions to other politicians in their campaigns for office. With PAC money, however, candidates also are able to travel around the country, hire staff and consultants, and develop mailing lists and fundraising appeals that will form the basis of their presidential campaigns. Some candidates even use their PAC money to pay for television and radio commercials in key primary states, even though the primaries are still months away.

One trick that many presidential candidates now employ in their early fundraising is to create leadership PACs in states with lax election laws.

According to the Federal Election Commission, the candidates who spent the most from their PACs in 2005–2006 were John McCain, $7.9 million; Barack Obama, $3.7 million; Hillary Rodham Clinton, $3.0 million; Mitt Romney, $2.9 million; John Edwards, $2.8 million; and Rudy Giuliani, $2.1 million.

Would-be presidential contenders also get involved in campaigning for candidates for Congress and state offices—flying into a candidate's district or state to make a speech, conduct interviews, or serve as the main attraction at a fund-raising event to benefit the candidate's campaign. Senator Clinton, for example, helped raise more than $15 million for Democratic candidates in 2006 by participating in over one hundred fundraising events.

What's more, candidates who have previously run for office often have money left over from their earlier races, which can give them a nice head start on the fund-raising trail. Hillary Rodham Clinton raised a whopping $51 million against a weak opponent in her 2006 New York Senate race, ending the race with $11 million she could transfer to her presidential campaign.

The Money Chase, Part II: The Exploratory Committee

If presidential candidates feel that they have a shot at winning the party nomination based on some of the activities described above, the next step is to file papers with the Federal Election Commission (FEC). This allows candidates to start raising money for polling and other campaign activities that will move them closer to a formal announcement.

Filing papers with the FEC usually coincides with announcements by candidates that they have formed an "exploratory committee" to investigate the possibility of a presidential run. Even if it's clear that the candidates have every intention of running for president, this exploratory committee provides an escape hatch should they decide the time's not right to run. Equally important, the announcement of an exploratory committee offers candidates an early shot of free publicity that can be repeated later on, when these candidates make it official that they are running for president.

In recent elections, the exploratory-committee announcement has become a campaign ritual in and of itself, with the contenders lining up for appearances on television talk shows and Sunday morning news programs to say they are taking this crucial first step toward running.

From the perspective of the officials at the FEC who regulate how candidates finance their campaigns, announcing an exploratory committee is the same thing as announcing a full-fledged campaign for the presidency. The reason is that once a candidate starts raising funds for a presidential bid, every amount counts toward the legal limits on contributions and spending, provided the candidate intends to participate in the public financing system. Whether the candidate says he or she is officially in the race is not an issue.

There's also a plus side to registering with the FEC. After this, money that the candidate raises helps him or her to qualify for matching funds from the federal government, if the candidate chooses to participate in the public funding system (see Chapter 5), which can really help a struggling campaign. To qualify for these matching funds, the candidate must raise more than $100,000 from individual contributions of $250 or less. That has to include at least $5,000 from each of twenty or more states.

Raising lots of money early in the game shows that a candidate is a serious contender and therefore helps raise even more money. Candidates have to file quarterly financial reports with the FEC, and these are public records. So all interested players can immediately see who is doing well in "the money primary."

For the 2008 race, the competition for funds got off to an early and high-stakes start. It's not surprising that the six candidates— three Republicans and three Democrats— whose leadership PACs doled out the most money in 2005–2006 (see page 97) were the same ones who were leading in the first quarter of official campaign fundraising, January to March 2007.

> *Raising lots of money early in the game shows that a candidate is a serious contender and therefore helps raise even more money.*

The big six out of the gate in 2007 were: Hillary Clinton, $36.0 million; Barack Obama, $25.8 million; Mitt Romney, $23.4 million; Rudy Giuliani, $16.6 million; John Edwards, $14.0 million; and John McCain, $13.0 million. These figures are much higher than in any previous election cycle: In the comparable period of the 2004 election, the biggest fundraiser was John Edwards with a paltry $7.4 million.

As soon as they became public, the 2007 numbers were scrutinized like a crystal ball by the media, the political pros, and half the blogosphere. One frequently made point: John McCain, once thought to be the Republican front-runner, did not do as well as his competitors, so he came out of this round looking wounded.

It used to be that candidates were in no particular hurry to declare their intention to run for president—or even to set up an exploratory committee. All an announcement accomplished was to invite federal scrutiny of the candidate's finances. If the candidate held a job that allowed him or her to travel the country and talk about issues that might be important in the presidential race, there was little incentive to make a formal declaration of candidacy because the candidate's travel would then have to be paid for by the campaign.

In recent years, however, candidates have realized that the sooner they get started raising the $50 million or more dollars they need to run a credible primary campaign, the better. And to start raising money, they have to file papers with the FEC. With donations for the primaries limited to $2,300 per person, the candidates will need to find at least 20,000 individual donors apiece. And they'll have to do it while their competitors for the party's nomination are knocking on many of the same folks' doors. Moreover, many candidates also seek out smaller contributions as well—they look better politically, plus a higher proportion will be eligible for federal matching funds.

Raising a great deal of money early—before the actual election year—has become essential to a successful campaign because of the "front-loaded" schedule of primary elections (see chapter 7). In 2008, a "super-primary" for twenty or more states is scheduled for February 5. That means that most of both parties' delegates will have been chosen by the end of February, so a candidate needs a big war chest by the fall of 2007 to pay for all that early campaigning.

Most of both parties' delegates will have been chosen by February 2008.

One note, however, about the importance of early fund-raising success—the Internet may be changing the rules of that game. As the Dean campaign, and later the Kerry campaign, showed, the Internet allows campaigns and allied players to raise millions of dollars faster than ever before. So early money and early endorsements may be less crucial in the future than they have been in recent election cycles—if a candidate can catch up quickly.

Competing for Talent: Lining Up Key Advisers and Staff

Another important task in the early going of a presidential campaign is to line up a campaign team. Often, candidates will compete for their party's top strategists and consultants—individuals believed to have the skills and the experience to help ensure the success of a candidate's campaign.

While presidential candidates often rely to some extent on staff members and advisers who have served them in previous stages of their career, it is considered crucial for key members of the team to have national campaign experience, as well as experience and contacts in key primary states.

Who's Who: The Campaign Team

Campaign staff members are often referred to as a presidential candidate's "handlers," and they include everyone from a campaign manager and press secretary to the advance staff that arranges candidate events just so—with a television-friendly backdrop, a happy, cheering crowd, and, of course, lots of American flags. Some of the key players on a presidential campaign team include the following:

- Campaign manager. Oversees the campaign operation
- Chief fundraiser. Oversees fund-raising and compliance with campaign finance laws
- Press secretary. Manages relations with the news media
- Pollster. Conducts polls to track the candidate's support, test the candidate's message, and identify key issues that concern voters
- Director of online communications. A position that has grown exponentially in importance; handles not only candidate Web sites and related e-mail, but also blogs, presence on social networking sites, YouTube, and more
- Consultants. Typically, the most important is the media consultant, who helps plan media campaigns and buy advertising. Other consultants advise on direct mail, fundraising, and get-out-the-vote.

Of course, these are just the top advisers, and a real campaign team includes hundreds, and often thousands, more. Other key players are the campaign volunteers throughout the country who help organize local events, distribute bumper stickers and buttons, and support the candidate at the local level. And don't forget the candidate's "brain-trust" advisers—the academics and current and former government officials whom the candidate will call on to help shape his or her policy proposals.

The Republican and Democratic parties have in recent elections shown some differences in the way they structure their campaign staffs. Democratic campaign organizations tend to reflect key constituencies within the party—African Americans, women, Latinos, youth. They also designate people to do outreach to specific sectors, such as Hollywood and business. Republican campaigns are not so clearly divided by constituency. While they have outreach staff for particular groups, Republican campaign staffs tend to be more homogeneous. Both parties also have state liaisons, particularly in key primary states.

The fact is that a presidential campaign today involves huge numbers of people. A big challenge in the early going is to start building the organization that will put all these people to work as effectively as possible.

Making It Official: The Announcement

In this age of television campaigning, you can bet that a contender for the office of president of the United States is not going to just appear at a press conference on Capitol Hill or somewhere equally unexciting and say, "I'm running."

A presidential candidate's formal announcement often looks like a homecoming rally, with cheering crowds, banners, balloons, and emotional appeals to family, home, and country. More often than not, the candidates return to the places where they were born or grew up so they can show they're normal Americans and haven't forgotten their roots.

Even though the media and the public usually know exactly what will be said at the announcement, the candidate's campaign makes the most of the opportunity to rouse the troops, highlight the candidate's unique qualifications and background, and offer a compelling vision for the country's future.

The announcement provides the candidate with a great opportunity for free publicity, as reporters and television crews from throughout the country draw attention to the candidate's bid for the presidency. Even for long-shot candidates who have little chance of winning any primaries, the announcement provides the "fifteen minutes of fame" that artist Andy Warhol said would someday be achieved by everyone.

After the Early Going: A Winnowing of the Field

By the end of the year preceding the presidential election—for the 2008 election, that means the end of 2007—the field of contenders for the party nominations usually has narrowed. If a candidate has failed to attract enough money and other support to mount a competitive race, the best thing to do now is to bow out instead of driving one's campaign further into debt.

In fact, with the accelerated schedule of the 2008 race and the increased need for huge piles of cash ASAP, some candidates who at first seemed clearly interested left the field before campaigning at all. Among those: former Virginia Governor Mark Warner, Senator Bill Frist, R-Tenn., and Iowa Governor Tom Vilsack.

Jimmy Carter famously won the Democratic nomination in 1976 by carefully building a low-budget grassroots campaign in Iowa to win the Iowa caucuses, then winning New Hampshire, and next broadening his support. It's very unlikely that type of strategy could succeed in 2008, because of the accelerated primary schedule and the enormous demand for funds.

Some observers fear that we are seeing the demise, or at least the decline, of a cherished ritual in presidential elections known as "retail" campaigning. That is, in the earliest stages of the race for their party's nomination, candidates would spend hundreds of hours in Iowa and New Hampshire, talking to ordinary people around kitchen tables and local diners. Voters would have a chance to "kick the tires," to ask questions based on their concerns, and see the candidates react face to face.

CAMPAIGN POLLING: FISHING FOR OPINION

For today's presidential candidates, polling has become an indispensable campaign tool from the early phases of the election onward. All major candidates employ professional pollsters to keep their fingers on the pulse of public opinion through telephone surveys and other methods. How do candidates use polls?

- To judge their chances of winning
- To identify issues voters care about
- To test campaign messages before they are incorporated into advertising and speeches
- To find out which voter groups—for example, the young, seniors, women, or residents of the Southeast—are most and least likely to support the candidate
- To figure out whether they are connecting with voters and whether their advertising and other campaigning are having the desired effect—namely, to attract support

The candidates' polls are rarely made public. They are normally used within the campaigns to help shape and refine campaign strategy, to sharpen the candidates' messages, and to determine what issues they should focus on. For example, if polling finds that a candidate's support among women voters is lacking, then the candidate might start to focus on issues that the campaign's polls say women care about.

The bottom line is that for better or worse, what a presidential candidate says in speeches, interviews, and advertising has been thoroughly tested before you, the voter, hear it. In the high-stakes game of presidential politics, it's rare for a candidate to say or do much at all without first consulting the polls (see chapter 4 for more).

It may be that in 2008, the Internet supersedes the traditional retail campaign. In any event, with the February 5 "mega-primary" coming so soon after Iowa and New Hampshire, candidates may feel the need to spend precious days in New York, California, and Florida, rather than chewing the fat in a snowbound New Hampshire cafe.

Another key aspect of the winnowing process is the series of debates within the parties. (These debates are distinct from the more heavily publicized debates between the two major party nominees that take place in the autumn before the November general election.) The intra-party debates take place in the months before the primaries and caucuses begin. The Republican Party scheduled ten debates between May 2007 and January 2008, with ten candidates participating in the initial lineup. The Democrats planned twelve debates between April 2007 and January 2008, with eight candidates participating in the first debate. (Cautionary note: both the schedule and the number of participants are likely to change.) Because the debates are televised, they give the parties' voters an excellent chance to observe their candidates in action before the first primary votes are cast.

In the high-stakes game of presidential politics, it's rare for a candidate to say or do much at all without first consulting the polls.

THE BATTLE FOR ENDORSEMENTS

Presidential candidates crave approval, and endorsements give them exactly that. Throughout the campaign, candidates are constantly battling for the endorsements of key individuals and organizations, including party leaders in key states, celebrities, religious leaders, union and police officials, newspaper editorial writers, and more.

Endorsements by prominent individuals and organizations provide the candidates with an opportunity to step before the news cameras and show that their campaigns are legitimate and that they are attracting support in key places. For voters, endorsements can provide added rationale for supporting a particular candidate—for example, if you're a steelworker and your union has thrown its weight behind Candidate X, or if you're concerned about the environment and one or more environmental groups have endorsed Candidate Y.

CHAPTER 7

The Primaries and Caucuses

It used to be that a political party's nominee for president was selected by influential party members at the party's national convention—generally after a lot of wheeling and dealing in smoke-filled rooms. Realizing that this was not a very democratic way to choose a major-party presidential candidate, the Democratic and Republican parties have over the last half century opened up the process to voters. The result is today's often confusing schedule of primaries and caucuses (see the primary season calendar, page 119-120), which makes voters—and not party leaders—the VIPs in choosing the parties' presidential nominees.

How It Works: Choosing the Delegates

The official role of the primaries and caucuses is to select delegates to the parties' national conventions held during the summer. Even in states where primary voters check off the presidential candidate of their choice, they are actually voting for delegates who support that candidate and will go to the convention representing the voters' preferences. In other words, a vote for Candidate X is actually a vote for Delegate Y, who in turn pledges to vote for Candidate X at the party convention.

The official role of the primaries and caucuses is to select delegates to the parties' national conventions held during the summer.

Because of the primaries and caucuses, the function of conventions in recent decades has not been to choose a nominee from among several contenders, but simply to ratify the choices that voters have already made. It's not impossible to imagine a situation in which the choice of presidential candidate had to be decided at the convention, but it's very unlikely. In large part, this is because once a contender seems likely to win the nomination, party activists unify around the candidate to create a united front for the coming general election. This unity building is usually emphasized at the party's convention. (See chapter 8 for more on what happens at the party gatherings.) It is possible that the accelerated primary schedule for 2008 will create a different dynamic in delegate selection—more on that later.

Different states have different ways of selecting delegates to the national conventions. Making it even more confusing, Republicans and Democrats often do things differently—even in the same state. In recent years, the presidential primary election has become the most common way for voters to have their say. The other main option for choosing delegates is the caucus, where party members meet at the local level to make their preferences known.

In recent years, the presidential primary election has become the most common way for voters to have their say.

Primary Education: What Is a Primary?

In a primary election, voters go to the polls to choose among a party's presidential candidates—or among would-be delegates who have pledged to support specific candidates at the party's national convention. Primaries were conceived early in the twentieth century as one way to take power away from the "party machines" and give the people a role in the nominating process. The primary grew in popularity in the 1970s. In 1960, sixteen states held primaries; by 1980 that had jumped to thirty-five states. In 2008, the Democrats and Republicans each planned to hold primary elections in more than forty-three states and the District of Columbia.

Primary Terminology

When you're following the news reports and political commentary during primary season, it helps to have an understanding of some of the terms used to describe the different types of primaries. In practice, though, states have many different rules about how primaries are conducted. Here are the main types:

- Closed Primary. Only voters registered with the party can vote in that party's primary. Held by about fifteen states.
- Open primary. The most common type of primary, held by about twenty-seven states. Voters can choose to vote in a party's primary, even if they are not registered with this party. In some states, primaries are open to independents but closed to those registered with other parties. In other states, the primaries are open to all voters. Party leaders tend to dislike this type of primary, because it allows voters outside the party to influence the selection of a nominee.
- Advisory primary. Sometimes derisively called a "beauty contest" primary. A few states let voters express a preference for which candidate they like best, independent of selecting convention delegates. Delegates are then chosen through other means, such as caucuses or conventions.

Primary elections are run differently in different states. In some states, voters mark the candidate they prefer—and delegates to the convention are allocated depending on the popular vote. This is often referred to as a direct presidential preference primary. In other cases, voters see on their ballot the names of the delegates, though the delegates are identified on the ballot as preferring a certain candidate or as uncommitted. This is known as an indirect presidential preference primary.

In some states, the primary is "binding" on the delegates—that is, the delegate promises to vote for the candidate he or she is pledged to, at least on the first ballot at the convention. In other states, the rules are less strict.

In addition, some primaries are "winner-take-all," so that whichever candidate receives the most popular votes gets all the state's delegates. Much more common is the "proportional representation" primary, where delegates are awarded roughly in proportion to their popular vote. A candidate who gets 20 percent of the vote, for example, will win about 20 percent of the state's delegates. All Democratic primaries follow the proportionality principle.

If you're interested in what kind of primary your state holds, the National Association of Secretaries of State maintains a Web site (www.nass.org) with links to election information provided by the secretaries of state in all fifty states.

A Primary Alternative: What's a Caucus?

In 2008, a very large majority of delegates in both major parties will be chosen by primaries. But states that don't hold primaries generally convene caucuses as a way to get voters involved in deciding on the party nominees. A caucus is a gathering of voters from the same party at the precinct level; a precinct is the smallest electoral district within a county. Caucuses tend to attract no more than 10 percent of the eligible voters; primaries often get 20 percent or more. In Washington state in 2000, for example, caucuses attracted 60,000 participants, while 1.3 million people voted in the state's primaries.

Caucuses can be a neighborly experience, with people from an area meeting and talking about the merits of the different candidates. In some states, that experience is considered valuable and worth keeping, even though caucuses may seem old-fashioned in the twenty-first century.

Caucuses tend to attract no more than 10 percent of the eligible voters; primaries often get 20 percent or more.

Participants in a caucus vote on party platforms and policies and select delegates to the next-higher-level party convention. There may be two or three higher levels, including district or county and state. In a caucus state, all those who want to represent their state at one of the national conventions must first win election as a convention delegate at one of the caucuses.

Caucuses generally occur at a set time and date in locations throughout the state; thousands of caucus meetings can be happening all at once. Party rules require caucus dates, times, and locations to be publicized well in advance so voters can plan to attend. The conventional wisdom is that caucuses are won by the best-organized candidates—those who are able to mobilize large numbers of loyal supporters to attend the caucus meetings.

The Early States: Iowa and New Hampshire

Over the last several decades, two states have emerged as the early battlegrounds in the presidential primary season. Those are Iowa and New Hampshire, which by custom and party rule hold the first caucuses and primary, respectively, of the campaign season. The Iowa caucuses and New Hampshire primary have proven to be crucial tests for presidential candidates from both parties—so crucial, in fact, that potential candidates can be found in these states years before the election, getting an early start on schmoozing voters and party leaders alike.

The Iowa caucuses and New Hampshire primary have proven to be crucial tests for presidential candidates from both parties.

New Hampshire's first-in-the-nation primary has become a matter of state pride. In fact, New Hampshire law requires the state's primary to be held at least seven days before any similar contest elsewhere (caucuses don't count). In 2008, the Iowa caucuses will be held January 14 and the New Hampshire primary on January 22.

BEWARE THE STRAW POLL!

In the weeks and months leading up to the primary season, state parties and other organizations often hold "straw polls" that try to measure support for the various candidates among the party faithful. Don't pay much attention to the results: Straw polls are unscientific, unofficial surveys and usually reflect the opinions of people who've paid to attend a party function or other meeting. In fact, often a candidate's campaign will try to influence the straw poll results by filling the meeting with his or her supporters.

Why are these two states so important? Candidates who do well in the Iowa caucuses or the New Hampshire primary get a flood of early media attention and are instantly crowned by the media and others as their parties' front-runners, despite the fact that the overwhelming majority of Americans haven't voted yet. Iowa and New Hampshire often set the tone for the rest of the election, establishing certain candidates as the ones to beat and leaving others in the dust. All the hype aside, early victories in Iowa and New Hampshire don't necessarily mean a candidate has a lock on the party's nomination. Consider the following early primary winners who went on to defeat:

Year	Candidate	What Happened
2000	John McCain	The senator from Arizona won the Republican New Hampshire primary by nineteen points, but was soon overtaken by George W. Bush, who had better national organization and funding.
1996	Patrick Buchanan	The former White House official won the New Hampshire primary in an upset victory over Bob Dole, but it was Dole who went on to win the Republican nomination.
1988	Richard Gephardt	The Midwestern congressional leader placed first in the Iowa caucuses in a Democratic nomination fight that was won in the end by Michael Dukakis.
1980	George H. W. Bush (Bush senior)	The future president beat Ronald Reagan in the Republican Iowa caucuses, but had to settle for the vice presidency after Reagan won the party's nomination.

THE EXPECTATIONS GAME

The hype surrounding the early primaries often revolves around one thing: expectations. If a candidate who is considered a long shot rises out of the pack to place first or a close second or third, then it's reported in the press as a major victory. On the other hand, if a candidate has achieved "front-runner" status and is expected to win big but doesn't, then it's reported in the media as a setback for the candidate's campaign—and the media pundits and the other candidates all start suggesting that front-runner so-and-so has lost momentum.

Bob Dole, who had been crowned as the clear front-runner in the 1996 Republican contest, came in first in the Iowa caucuses. But he attracted only 26 percent of the vote—just three points ahead of the next candidate, Pat Buchanan. As a result, the media presented it as though Buchanan had won—he had beaten expectations—while Dole was on the ropes. Dole actually lost the next race, the New Hampshire primary, but he recovered over the next few weeks and went on to win the Republican nomination.

A Mega-Primary for 2008

The schedule of primary elections has been moving up in time since the 1980s. What used to be a gradual procession of primaries that stretched from February to June has now become a deluge of decision-making in January and early February.

What's the reason for this change of pace? The reason given by many state leaders is that they feel their states and their voters have been left out of the action because of their late primaries. By moving to February, they hope to gain more influence over the nomination process.

In addition, many state leaders became jealous of the special attention given by presidential candidates, the media, and the rest of the country to the early primary and caucus states, especially Iowa and New Hampshire. The early events are also quite lucrative for the states hosting them, because they attract not only the campaigns but also media from around the world.

As recently as 1992, California, which has more delegates than any other state, held its party primaries in June. But in 1996, the state moved its primaries up to March 26. And in 2008, California will hold its primary on February 5, along with around twenty other states, probably including delegate-rich Texas, New York, and Illinois.

With so many big states voting on February 5, the United States for the first time ever faces something resembling a national primary—and no one knows how this will play out.

Among the questions raised by the new schedule:

- Will the role of Iowa and New Hampshire increase or diminish? Traditionally, victories or better-than-expected showings gave candidates a boost in fundraising and a leg up on the next round of primaries. With such a short time between those early contests and the mega-primary February 5, will that still hold true?
- Will there still be time for the "retail" campaigning that Iowa and New Hampshire voters expect?
- How will candidates and their organizations balance spending face-time in Iowa and New Hampshire with the need to raise millions of dollars and build organizations across the United States?
- How will the February 5 mega-primary affect the "bandwagon effect" that has usually produced a party united behind clear winner before the end of the primary season?

The bandwagon effect, long observed by politicians and scholars, is based on a simple fact: People like to be on the winning team. So in previous elections, at least since the 1970s, as one candidate emerged with the strongest showing after several rounds of primaries, the media, political leaders, and voters all began to rally around the presumptive winner. Competitors dropped out, and by April the party was able to begin uniting around its nominee.

Will that still occur in 2008? Or, with several strong candidates competing in both major parties, will the mega-primary on February 5 produce no clear favorites? If that occurs, a competitive battle for the nomination could conceivably continue for months, even until the party convention.

A convention with more than one candidate in contention (it would be the first since 1952) would be exciting for fans of the political process. But you can be sure that party leaders, who prefer unity and predictability, would be quite unhappy with that scenario.

The bandwagon effect may also be weakened in 2008 by the rise of early voting in many states. Citizens are increasingly being allowed to vote early, either by sending in absentee ballots or stopping by special polling stations, weeks before the official election day. In Florida, for example—scheduled to vote one week after New Hampshire—47 percent of voters in 2006 cast either early or absentee ballots. If that pattern continues in 2008, most of those voters won't be affected by the New Hampshire returns: They'll already have voted when those returns come in.

On the other hand, if the parties' nominations are in fact decided in February, that will leave five months between the primary season and the convention—five months in which many voters might lose interest in the whole campaign. Candidates also receive no public funding during those five months, though that is not likely to be a factor in 2008. Probably, the winning candidate in both the Democratic and Republican party primary process will not have accepted public funds and will not be bound by the accompanying spending limits.

Some political thinkers believe that the various states' race to be the first in the primary schedule is counterproductive and is making the nominating process less involving for voters. One alternative proposal that has gotten some attention is having several regional primaries—say, for the South, Northeast, Midwest, and West—scheduled over several months. In order not to give any region a permanent advantage, the schedule could be rotated from one election to the next, so that the Southern primary might be first in 2012, the Western primary first in 2016, and so forth. The National Association of Secretaries of States—those are the state officials who generally run elections—favors this proposal.

Primary Participation: Who Votes in the Primaries?

There is no doubt that the primaries and caucuses have succeeded in getting voters more involved in selecting the major-party presidential nominees. But there are still problems. In fact, many people say we still have a long way to go before we achieve the goal of democratizing the presidential nomination process.

Why? Because voter participation is low in the primaries and especially in the caucuses compared to the general election in the fall. Typically, turnout in primaries is anywhere between one-tenth and one-half of the turnout for the November general election. The problem is exacerbated by the front-loaded primary schedule, since voters in the later contests often feel that there's not much point in voting—at least not in the presidential contest—because the nominee has already been determined.

Typically, turnout in primaries is anywhere between one-tenth and one-half of the turnout for the November general election.

Many people are worried less by the numbers of voters in the primary season than by the fact that the primaries and caucuses generally attract certain types of voters. Scholars have found, for example, that the average primary voter tends to be slightly better educated, more affluent, and older than the average voter in general elections. Primary voters also are more likely than the general election voter to be to have strong party ties and be further from the political center. For Republicans, this means that primary voters are more conservative than average; for Democrats, more liberal.

Thus, candidates often feel compelled to speak differently during the primaries and the general election. In the primaries, they will speak in a more partisan and ideological vein, to win over their party's true believers. During the general election, they often try to appeal to the political center, where the swing voters are—undecided voters who could go either way.

What's more, in a crowded primary field, the candidate who stands alone on the ideological spectrum gains an advantage. If five liberal Democrats and one conservative Democrat are running in New Hampshire, there's a good chance the five liberals will split that section of the electorate, and the lone conservative can then win.

Caucuses attract even fewer voters on a percentage basis than primary elections. And caucus voters, who might have to dedicate an entire evening to appearing at the caucus site for a public discussion of candidates and issues, tend to be even stronger partisans than voters in the party primaries.

Despite these drawbacks, there is widespread agreement that the primaries and caucuses are a definite improvement over the smoke-filled rooms and secret deals of the past. If the primary and caucus participants are not representative of the wider population, the answer may not be changing the system of primaries and caucuses. Rather, a better solution may be to convince more voters to show up and make their preferences known.

By skipping the primaries and caucuses, you leave it to others to decide whom you'll be voting for in the fall.

In other words, more voters need to hear the message that going to the polls in November is not enough. By skipping the primaries and caucuses, they're leaving it to others to decide whom they'll be voting for in the fall.

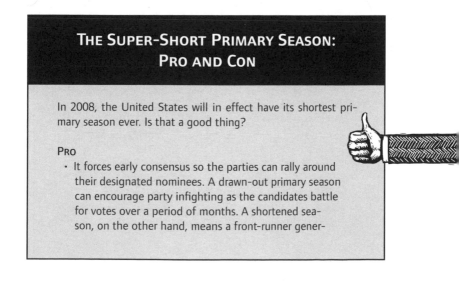

THE SUPER-SHORT PRIMARY SEASON: PRO AND CON

In 2008, the United States will in effect have its shortest primary season ever. Is that a good thing?

PRO
- It forces early consensus so the parties can rally around their designated nominees. A drawn-out primary season can encourage party infighting as the candidates battle for votes over a period of months. A shortened season, on the other hand, means a front-runner gener-

ally emerges early (probably by the end of February
in 2008). The party can then unite behind his or her
candidacy and start planning for the general election
instead of tearing itself apart.

· It avoids placing too much emphasis on voter senti-
ment in just one or two states. New Hampshire and
Iowa aren't necessarily representative of the country as
a whole. And yet these two states—which are racially
much whiter than the country as a whole—have had a
significant impact on presidential elections simply by
voting early. It might be better to cast a wider net and
give more voters and more states an early say in shaping
the course of the campaign.

· It rewards candidates with the strongest organizations. A
primary season in which more states vote early benefits
candidates who have worked hard to build support
throughout the country. A shorter primary season thus
makes it less likely that a candidate with regional or
"fringe" appeal will emerge as the one to beat.

Con

· It favors candidates with the most money. It used to
be that a presidential candidate could invest heavily in
a few early primary states, hoping that major money
would start coming in after a successful early showing.
Today, however, candidates need to campaign from the
start in a larger number of larger states. And that puts
pressure on the candidates to raise and spend more
money.

· It means more television ads and Internet emphasis, less
"retail" campaigning. It is impossible for candidates to
establish a personal presence in so many states in so
little time. The result: campaigns based on TV commercials, and less time for the voters to get to know the
candidates and vice versa.

· It creates a period of several months—between March
and the summer conventions—when voters lose interest in the election. In 2000, after primary campaigning
peaked in March, the number of people paying close
attention to the campaign dropped by 50 percent.

- It puts lesser-known candidates at a disadvantage. Twenty or thirty years ago, it was possible for relatively unknown candidates to do well in early contests in less populous states like Iowa and New Hampshire. This early success, in turn, could attract money, volunteers, and media attention to their campaigns and make them viable contenders for the party nomination. This has become almost impossible with the front-loaded primary schedule.
- Some observers dispute the notion that a shorter primary season will make Iowa and New Hampshire less important. With less time to learn about the candidates, they suggest, voters elsewhere may be more likely to follow the lead of the two earliest states.

Tentative Primary and Caucus Schedule for 2008

The following is a list of 2008 presidential primary and caucus dates for the fifty states, plus the District of Columbia, as of July 2007. Many of these dates are subject to change as states compete to schedule their primaries and caucuses as early as they can and Iowa and New Hampshire jockey to protect their status as the leadoff caucus state and primary state, respectively.

Some states are not included because they had not set their dates at the time this table was prepared. State dates that are under consideration but not yet finalized list the state in bold italics. States with an asterisk (*) beside their name have indicated that their contest could move to another date but have not provided alternative dates.

JANUARY 2008
- January 8: District of Columbia**
- January 14: Iowa (caucuses)*
- January 19: Nevada (caucuses)

- January 22: New Hampshire (primary)*, Wyoming (GOP caucuses)***
- January 29: Florida, South Carolina (Dem primary)

FEBRUARY 2008
- February (Date TBD): Michigan
- February 1: Maine (GOP)
- February 2: South Carolina (GOP primary)
- February 5: Alabama, Alaska, Arizona , Arkansas, California, Colorado (caucuses), Connecticut, Delaware, Georgia, Idaho (Dem), Illinois, Minnesota (GOP), Missouri, New Jersey, New Mexico (Dem), New York, North Dakota, Oklahoma, Tennessee, Utah
- February 7: Hawaii (GOP)
- February 9: Louisiana
- February 10: Maine (Dem)
- February 12: Maryland, Virginia
- February 19: Hawaii (Dem), Washington, Wisconsin

MARCH 2008
- March 4: Massachusetts, Ohio, Texas, Vermont
- March 8: Wyoming (Dem)
- March 11: Mississippi
- March 18: Rhode Island

APRIL 2008
- April 22: Pennsylvania

MAY 2008
- May 6: Indiana, North Carolina
- May 10: Wyoming (Dem caucuses)
- May 13: Nebraska, West Virginia
- May 20: Kentucky, Oregon
- May 27: Idaho

JUNE 2008
- June 3: Montana, South Dakota

State may move their primary date but has not provided alternate dates.
*** Nonbinding primary*
*** Wyoming moves if New Hampshire does*

Note: Kansas has opted not to have a presidential primary in 2008.
Source: National Association of Secretaries of State. Visit www.nass.org and www.VOTE411.org for the most current primary and caucus dates.

CHAPTER 8

Conventions

The national party conventions mark the official turning point in the presidential campaign from the primary season to the general election in the fall. Although it is generally widely known for months before who the presidential nominee will be, the convention allows the party to put aside any intra-party jockeying and squabbles that occurred during the primaries, unite behind its nominee, define itself for the voters, and set the tone for the fall offensive.

In recent years, the interest of the parties in staging controversy-free and television-friendly conventions has caused both voters and the media to lose interest in the events. Before the 1950s, conventions could easily turn into high-drama affairs as the parties battled within themselves over key issues, and the selection of the party's nominees for president and vice president wasn't certain until the final voting. But today, the conventions have turned into what one television anchor has called infomercials for the national parties. They are events that are scripted with one thing in mind: marketing the party and its candidates to the American electorate.

What's It All About? The Function of the National Conventions

Marketing isn't the only function of the conventions. In a formal sense, the conventions are the highest, most important source of authority for a national party. That is, the conventions are officially the top decision-making body of the parties.

But this way of looking at the conventions is somewhat old-fashioned. In reality, most of the important decisions about the direction of the party and the identity of the party's nominees for president and vice president have already been made by the time the convention starts—by the nominee, the nominee's top political strategists, and the national committee of the party.

Nonetheless, the party conventions do play some important formal roles. In addition to nominating the president and vice president, conventions officially establish party rules and priorities for the four years between presidential elections (see chapter 3 for more on how the parties work). The conventions are the only time the parties gather at the national level, and so there's business to be done both on and off the convention floor. The major items on the convention agenda:

- Nominate candidates for president and vice president. This is the convention function that gets the most attention, even though the party nominees are usually known well in advance. (The last contested party convention was the 1976 Republican convention, in which Ronald Reagan unsuccessfully challenged Gerald Ford for the nomination.) Most often, the role of the national party convention today is merely to ratify the choice that the voters made during primary and caucus season by nominating the top vote getter among the party's presidential contenders. In choosing the vice presidential nominee, delegates invariably go along with their presidential nominee's choice of a running mate, whose identity is invariably known in advance.

- Adopt a national party platform. The platform is a declaration of the party's principles and its positions on important issues confronting the nation. Although it is not binding on candidates, the platform establishes a tone and a direction for the party's efforts at all levels of government. "Platform fights" can still erupt over the party's positions on hot-button issues such as trade or abortion, but the parties generally try to smooth out the differences and encourage compromise in the interest of demonstrating party unity.

+ Adopt the rules that govern the party for the next four years. (This is especially true for the Republicans; the Democratic Party's national committee, which meets regularly, can also change party rules.) The conventions offer a chance to discuss and approve the rules governing how the parties function. Conventions can consider changes in party rules and procedures on issues from the selection of national convention delegates to the composition of the party's national committee. Convention delegates also elect national committee members and convention officers.

+ Rally the party faithful. The convention is also an opportunity to recognize all the people who have worked hard for the party and given their time and money to help it succeed. And it is a time to try to make sure that the party's supporters are still behind it and will continue to work for the party and its candidates during the upcoming election and beyond.

Despite the many functions they serve, the conventions may be in for some changes. In May 2007, Democratic National Committee Chairman Howard Dean told a Denver journalist, "We've got to change the way we do conventions in this country. I'm looking to try to make this a transitional convention, in the sense that the day of the $50 to $60 million convention is coming to a close." Dean critiqued the traditional convention as being exclusively "one-way communication" from the party outward to the voter, failing to engage voters. As chairman of the DNC, Dean may have considerable influence over the shape of the next Democratic convention.

The Delegates: Who Are All These People?

Convention delegates used to be a fairly homogeneous group of business and labor leaders, wealthy individuals, and politicians—and most of them were white, male, and middle age or older. But then in the 1970s and 1980s, the parties opened up the delegate selection process in an effort to populate the conventions with more women, minorities, and young people. The Democrats even went so far as to require that each state's delegation to the national convention be equally divided between women and men.

In 2008, the Republican convention will seat about twenty-five hundred delegates, and the Democratic convention about forty-three hundred. Many "alternates" also attend the conventions; they have most of the privileges of delegates, but do not have voting rights.

> *In 2008, the Republican convention will seat about twenty-five hundred delegates, and the Democratic convention about forty-three hundred.*

Although the state delegations at the Democratic convention are larger than those at the Republican, both parties base the number of delegates per state on some combination of the state's population and the relative strength of the party in the state—for example, by looking at how well the party's nominee did in that state in the last presidential election.

As described in chapter 7, convention delegates are selected based on the results of the primaries and caucuses in their states, with most of the delegates coming to the convention pledged to support a specific candidate. In addition, the Democrats have uncommitted "superdelegates," who automatically get a vote at the convention because of their position in the party. Superdelegates include all sitting Democratic governors and members of Congress, plus members of the Democratic National Committee. They account for about one in five of all delegates at the Democratic convention.

Instead of superdelegates, the Republicans award states a specific number of "at-large" delegates of their own choosing. The number of at-large delegates per state varies depending on the relative strength of the party in the state—for example, whether or not the state voted for the Republican candidate in the last presidential election, whether or not it has a Republican governor, and the percentage of Republicans in the state legislature and the state's congressional delegation. At the GOP convention, a little more than one-quarter of the delegates will be at large.

Of course, the delegates aren't the only people at the conventions. There are also hordes of media representatives and television pundits, along with issue advocates, from environmentalists and farmers to labor union and business representatives, who all want the party to embrace their issues.

You won't see these people on the convention floor, though; their lobbying usually takes place behind the scenes at strategy meetings and after-hours receptions.

CONVENTIONS AND MONEYED INTERESTS

For every election since 1976, under the Federal Election Campaign Act, the major parties have received funds from the federal treasury to pay for their nominating conventions. As with the campaigns themselves, the idea was that federal funding would reduce the influence of special interests—like wealthy individuals, corporations, and unions—over the parties.

This new system worked just fine through the 1980s. But through a series of rulings, the Federal Election Commission (FEC) allowed interest groups to donate as much money as they want to the "host committees" running the conventions. The FEC allowed this, even though federal funding of the conventions was indexed for inflation—from $4.4 million in 1980 to $14.9 million in 2004.

Since the 1980s, the big moneyed interests have ramped up their contributions to the conventions enormously, to the point where private money now dwarfs the public funding. This trend increased even more after 2002, when the McCain-Feingold campaign reform law (BCRA) cut off the flow of soft money to the parties. Now, donating to the convention "host committees" is one of the few legal ways for corporations and unions to give large amounts of money to the parties.

In 1980, private contributions to the conventions were a modest 13 percent of the public funding. That percentage increased to 155 percent in 1996 and 333 percent in 2004. Most likely, the percentage will be even higher in 2008. Private interests gave $106 million to the Republican convention and $64.5 million to the Democratic convention in 2004. Much of the private funding goes for extravagant parties and celebrations, not the basic business of the conventions.

While some reform groups have petitioned the FEC to change its convention funding rules, those permissive, "spend-all-you-want" policies remain in place as of mid-2007.

Conventional Wisdom: "My Kind of Town"

The Democratic and Republican Party conventions are prestigious and economically important events, so cities compete to attract the conventions by offering to share the costs.

However, the economic impact of a convention is difficult to compute with any precision or reliability. For example, while Boston's mayor predicted that the 2004 Democratic convention held in his city would net $154 million for the local economy, a local think tank estimated after the convention that, taking into account the many costs of the convention for residents and workers, the city actually netted just $15 million.

Where a party holds its convention can make a political statement. Until 2004, the Republican Party had never had a convention in New York City, but it did so in August 2004. Why? In part because New York City had a Republican mayor, so it was politically friendly territory, despite its generally Democratic voting record. Probably more important, New York City had suffered heavily from the terrorist attacks of September 11, 2001. So holding the convention in the Big Apple both expressed support for the city and reminded voters that the Bush administration had launched a vigorous military response to the terrorist attacks. That was probably a smart political move.

Another kind of message is being sent by the Democratic Party, which is holding its 2008 convention in Denver. While in recent presidential elections, the Democratic Party has done poorly in the mountain West, having the convention in Denver shows that the party plans to contest races all over the region. That fits in with party chairman (and former candidate) Howard Dean's "50-state strategy" of establishing a Democratic presence in every part of the country.

The Democratic National Convention in Denver will take place from August 25 to 28. The Republicans will hold their national convention in Minneapolis-St. Paul from September 1 to 4.

The Scripted Convention: "Boring Is Good"

Until the 1950s, it was common for the parties to have "brokered" conventions, meaning that the nomination was up for grabs. Behind-the-scenes deals were made, votes were traded, and a compromise candidate was frequently chosen from the pack as the nominee.

Since 1952, however, when Republican Dwight Eisenhower and Democrat Adlai Stevenson faced each other in the general election after protracted wheeling and dealing at their party conventions, the choice of nominees has been pretty much a foregone conclusion.

We should note, however, that a brokered convention in 2008 is not impossible to imagine, especially with a primary schedule that may distribute delegates among several strong candidates. Both the Democratic and Republican conventions will have large numbers of delegates (mostly party honchos) who are not formally committed

CONVENTION LOWLIGHTS

Even though the conventions have not chosen the presidential nominee in decades, they still occasionally make news or show an interesting aspect of the party or candidate. And then there are those conventions that give political honchos nightmares.

- 1968 DEMOCRATIC NATIONAL CONVENTION. A convention planner's worst nightmare, the 1968 Democratic national convention in Chicago erupted into chaos when protests over the Vietnam War led to bloody street battles between demonstrators and police.
- 1972 DEMOCRATIC NATIONAL CONVENTION. Even though party strategists had planned for nominee George McGovern to deliver his acceptance speech in prime time (around 10 P.M. Eastern Time), a floor dispute preceding the speech lasted well into the early morning. By the time McGovern finally stepped up to the podium, most of the television audience had gone to bed.
- 1992 REPUBLICAN NATIONAL CONVENTION. Patrick Buchanan and other convention speakers drew such a hard line on various cultural and religious issues that it irritated mainstream voters watching at home, who later told pollsters they saw the Republican message as intolerant and exclusionary.

to any candidate. And when a candidate drops out of the race, as often happens during the primary season, the candidate's delegates are usually released to vote for someone else.

In all recent elections, however, the job of the convention delegates has not been to choose the party's standard-bearer but to confirm the choice that voters throughout the country made months before during the primaries and caucuses. The vice presidential nominee, too, has generally been selected before the convention starts.

According to the political parties, that's just fine. The way they see it, the fewer surprises, the better. As Democratic consultant James Carville said about his party's then-upcoming 1996 convention, "Boring is good." Since the dawn of the television age, the conventions have been viewed by the parties as their best chance to connect with a national audience and to articulate what the party stands for. Anything that gets in the way of an orderly, television-friendly presentation of the party and its candidates is unwelcome.

The parties especially like the conventions because they give the parties and their candidates a chance to deliver their messages without interruption from journalists or opposing candidates. Partly as a result, the conventions temporarily give the public a more upbeat view of the campaigns.

> *Today's national party conventions are so scripted and stage-managed that they resemble a Broadway show more than a freewheeling political event.*

For example, the convention helped Democratic nominee John Kerry make a positive impression on people in 2004. Among those who said they watched some of the 2004 convention on TV, seven times as many said they thought better of Kerry from what they saw on TV than said they thought worse of him. Campaign professionals talk about the "bounce"—the increase in favorable poll ratings—that a party's candidates can get from a well-presented, upbeat convention.

Today's national party conventions are so scripted and stage-managed that they resemble a Broadway show more than a freewheeling political event. Speakers are chosen based on political considerations; they submit their remarks in advance for review by party officials; key events are scheduled for prime time, when the most viewers will be watching on television; and potential controversies are (hopefully) swept under the rug so the show can go on without a hitch.

This doesn't mean the conventions aren't worth watching; voters can actually learn a good deal about a party and its candidates by tuning in. Many viewers say that they learned something about the candidates and their positions from the TV coverage.

Many voters make up their minds which candidate they plan to vote for during the conventions.

People are also more likely to talk about the candidates during the conventions.

In addition, many voters make up their minds which candidate they plan to vote for during the conventions. At the time of the 2000 conventions, the number of Americans who said they were undecided about their choice of candidate dropped from 55 percent to 41 percent.

The conventions also get people talking about the election. According to one survey, during the Democratic convention of 2004, 42 percent of young adults participated in a conversation about the election on a given day, up from 15 percent before the convention.

The Role of the Media: The Conventions As News Events

Despite the parties' efforts to make their national conventions more television-friendly, in recent years the television networks have drastically cut back their coverage of the events. In 1976, the three major TV networks broadcast an average of twenty-five hours of coverage of each party convention. By 1984, that had fallen to twelve hours, and by 2004 it was down to three hours. Not surprisingly, the number of hours the average American household watches the conventions on television has also plummeted.

The reason for the decline has been a lack of real news. After just two days at the Republican National Convention in San Diego in 1996, Ted Koppel, then host of ABC's Nightline, announced he was returning home to New York. "This convention is more of an info-mercial than a news event," he said. "Nothing surprising has hap-pened. Nothing surprising is anticipated." That's likely to be even more true in 2008.

Whereas the television networks used to provide "gavel-to-gavel" coverage of the conventions, today they broadcast only selected events, such as the nominee's acceptance speech. And they regularly cut away from the convention proceedings to talk about what's hap-pening with their correspondents and expert pundits, or to present their own interviews with party leaders.

Sometimes, the way the media covers today's conventions is a good thing—it can mean the viewers are more informed about what's going on than the actual delegates on the convention floor. But often the networks focus too much on convention politics and don't give voters the information they need to make an informed decision come November—for example, by examining the party platforms and how they differ.

For people who want to learn more about the parties, candidates, and conventions, cable news networks such as CNN, C-SPAN, and MSNBC offer more extensive live convention coverage. Plus, there are countless Web sites maintained by the media, the par-ties, and other organizations that feature daily convention cover-age and the full text of speeches, along with information about the party platforms, candidate biographies, and more (see chapter 4 for a guide to election-related Web sites). The blogosphere also goes at the conventions full force, dissecting every development and its meaning.

And despite the cold shoulder from the television networks, there is generally convention coverage in the newspapers and other "tra-ditional media." After all, the national party conventions—along with the candidates' debates—are the biggest media events of the presidential campaign.

Convention Highlights: A Viewer's Guide

There's always a lot going on at the national party conventions, but a few key events will give you a good idea of how the party and its candidate are trying to present themselves to the voters.

The Image Machine

As the conventions have become more of a marketing event, the role of video, music, and other media have increased. A smart campaign manager will use all possible elements, including the candidate's words and family, to create an attractive image the public will buy. A noted example was the Democratic convention of 1992, when candidate Bill Clinton, much disparaged as "slick Willie," was repackaged as "the man from Hope." A video that showed the teenage Clinton shaking hands with his hero, President John F. Kennedy, helped make the sale.

What to look for: Image-making can be fun, even moving, to watch, but keep in mind that the purpose of the presentation is to sell the candidate to the voters. Ask yourself whether the candidate is being presented realistically and whether thoughtful solutions to the nation's problems are even discussed.

The Keynote Address

The keynote address is the first highlight of the convention. Presented by a prominent or up-and-coming politician in the party, the keynote serves to rally the party around a specific set of themes and issues and to convey the party's message in a compelling way.

What to look for: Often, the selection of the keynoter is as important a statement of the party's goals and direction as the speech itself. The keynoter might represent a state or region that the party feels it needs to capture—for example, the South or California—or perhaps an important segment of the electorate that the party wants to reach, such as women, minorities, or younger voters.

Giving the keynote can be a big boost for a politician who's seeking national recognition. At the Democratic convention of 2004, Senate candidate Barack Obama made such a positive impression with his keynote address that he was instantly given status as a rising star in the party.

The Nomination of the Vice Presidential Candidate

Conventions invariably honor the wishes of the presidential nominee in the choice of a running mate, so the nomination of the vice presidential candidate is a formality.

THE VICE PRESIDENCY:
MORE IMPORTANT THAN YOU THINK

Think it doesn't matter who's number two on the ticket? Think again. For one thing, recent vice presidents have played a more active role than their predecessors in policy making. Vice President Al Gore helped to define the Clinton administration's environmental policies and spearheaded the drive to "re-invent government" by making it more efficient. And Vice President Dick Cheney played a key role in energy policy and in setting the course for the war in Iraq during the administration of George W. Bush.

What's more, as the next in line if something should happen to the president, the vice president better be ready to lead. The American public has been reminded again and again that it matters who's vice president. In the last fifty years, President Kennedy died in office, President Nixon resigned, President Reagan was shot, and President Clinton faced an impeachment trial in the U.S. Senate.

Another reason to pay attention to the vice presidential nominees: The vice presidency is considered the perfect platform for launching a presidential campaign. Al Gore and George Bush the elder are recent examples of vice presidents who ran for their former bosses' jobs. Dick Cheney, George W. Bush's vice president, passed on a presidential bid, but he's the exception to the rule.

The presidential nominee's speech is considered the most important speech of the campaign.

What to look for: The selection of a vice presidential nominee usually is driven by an interest in balancing the party's ticket for maximum vote-getting potential. A presidential candidate from the Northeast, for example, might select a running mate from the South or West, and a candidate from the party's liberal or conservative wing might choose someone with more mainstream appeal. The ticket can also be balanced in terms of expertise, as when Texas Governor George W. Bush, with little foreign affairs experience, chose as his running mate former Secretary of Defense Dick Cheney.

The Acceptance Speeches

It used to be that candidates didn't even go to the party conventions. But Franklin D. Roosevelt broke this tradition and flew to Chicago in 1932 to accept the Democratic Party nomination, and both party's nominees have done so since then. Both the vice presidential and the presidential nominees give acceptance speeches on the convention's final day.

What to look for: The presidential nominee's speech is considered the most important speech of the campaign, setting the tone for the fall election, laying out issue priorities, and identifying key differences between the parties.

CHAPTER 9

The General Election Campaign

After winning the Republican Party's nomination in 1860, Abraham Lincoln was elected to the presidency without ever leaving his hometown of Springfield, Illinois, and without making a single speech. One hundred years later, Republican nominee Richard Nixon traveled 65,000 miles, made 212 speeches, visited all fifty states—and lost. The day of the "front-porch" presidential campaign that was the custom during Lincoln's time is long gone. Today's general election contest is an elaborate production, with the candidates and their supporters crisscrossing the country and blanketing the airwaves with poll-tested political commercials.

With the primaries and the conventions behind them, the goal of the presidential candidates during the fall is to appeal to as many different kinds of people in as many different ways as possible. To accomplish this in a country where more than 200 million individuals are eligible to vote is a staggering task. It requires an effective national organization, enormous discipline on the part of the candidates and their campaigns, and large numbers of staff and volunteers, not to mention a great deal of money.

Campaign Strategy, Part I: A Shift to the Center

The fall brings with it a number of strategic decisions for the candidates and their campaign organizations. But perhaps the most

WHAT'S A WEDGE ISSUE?

A man named Willie Horton became famous during the 1988 presidential campaign as a tragic and misleading symbol of Democratic candidate Michael Dukakis's policies as governor of Massachusetts. While on furlough from a Massachusetts prison, Horton had raped a woman and held her and her husband hostage. Dukakis's opponents used the Horton story to paint the governor as "soft on criminals."

The Willie Horton story is an example of how presidential candidates and their supporters work to identify and take advantage of "wedge issues." These are issues that drive a wedge between segments of the electorate and create doubts about an opponent's policies and beliefs, even among many of the opponent's supporters. Crime is a perennial wedge issue, with candidates regularly staking out hard-line stands on the death penalty, parole for prisoners, and other topics. Other wedge issues that presidential candidates have used in recent years to appeal to voters' emotions include prayer in schools, flag burning, gun control, and abortion. Issues that have broad appeal and are non-controversial, such as good education and a strong economy, do not lend themselves to being used as wedge issues.

important decision facing the candidates as they approach the general election season is how to refine their message so it resonates with a majority of the American electorate.

Why tinker with a message that worked fine in the primaries? Because in the primaries the candidates were appealing to voters of their own parties, but now they are trying to connect with a much larger audience. This means they need to adopt a more mainstream message, a message with broad appeal, beyond the party faithful.

"Shifting to the center," as it is called, is often a tightrope walk for the candidates, because they don't want to offend their primary supporters or make it appear as though they are abandoning their earlier commitments. In 2000, for example, George W. Bush had appealed to the Republican Party's religious conservatives in successfully fending off the challenge of a more centrist and reformist candidate, Senator John McCain. In the fall election, his slogan "compassionate conservatism" and his proposal for a limited prescription drug plan for seniors helped him make the case to moderate voters that he was not a hard-line right-winger.

Many observers of presidential politics say that the interest in crafting messages and themes with the broadest possible appeal makes the candidates overly cautious in what they say. Bold statements on important policy issues will only antagonize certain segments of the electorate, the thinking goes, so the candidates are content to speak in generalities as much as they can.

One noted example of a candidate getting too specific about what he'd do in office was Democratic nominee Walter Mondale, in 1984. Running against the incumbent, Ronald Reagan, Mondale paid a price for predicting that he would have to raise taxes if he became president. His loss at the polls served as a warning to future presidential candidates that sometimes glowing generalities go down easier than precise but controversial proposals.

Of course, the candidates' interest in saying as little as possible about some of the critical issues facing the country is in direct conflict with the voters' need to know the candidates' true beliefs. This is why the presidential debates, media interviews, and other unscripted campaign events are such an important part of the fall campaign— they provide the news media and the voters with a chance to ask the candidates challenging questions about where they stand.

Campaign Strategy, Part II: Targeting a Candidate's Appeal

At the same time that the candidates have to reach out to a broad cross section of the American electorate, they must also decide how to target their campaigning for maximum effect. Because of the limited amounts of time and money available to candidates, it simply isn't possible for them to wage a full-fledged campaign in every state or among all voters. This means that the candidates have to focus on specific states and regions that they feel will be decisive in determining the winner of the election. For a well-run campaign, that means keeping your eye on the Electoral College votes required to win the election. It also means that the candidates have to target their appearances and their advertising to specific groups of voters. To help cover the many places they can't visit, candidates rely on state and local party organizations to generate interest in the campaign and turn out the vote.

Targeting Key States …

Under the Electoral College system, almost all of the states award their electoral votes on a winner-take-all basis, so that the candidate who receives the most popular votes in a state receives all of that state's electoral votes. (In two states, Maine and Nebraska, electoral votes may be divided among the candidates.) Because the number of electoral votes each state receives is based on its population, the most populous states—such as California, New York, Texas, Florida, Illinois, and Pennsylvania—are sometimes high-intensity battlegrounds in the general election. In practice, these states often are not, when they are considered a sure bet for one candidate or another. In 2004, for example, the state of New York was considered a safe state for Democrat John Kerry, so neither major candidate did much campaigning there (see chapter 10 for more on the Electoral College system and a chart of electoral votes per state).

> *Candidates have to focus on specific states and regions that they feel will be decisive in determining the winner of the election.*

WHAT'S A SWING STATE?

The candidates generally focus their campaigning on "swing states" that could go either way in the presidential election. They are states where no candidate or party has a lock on the majority of voters, or where a crucial margin of voters is still undecided. In recent elections, Florida, Ohio, and Pennsylvania have been important swing states.

Candidates devote their energies to the largest states that they feel they have a chance of winning. At the same time, they tend to make only token appearances in states where they are assured of victory, while conceding those states where their chances are slim. This emphasis on swing states has led in recent presidential elections to a noticeable split in the campaign. Voters in targeted states are exposed to a flood of television ads every day and get lots of campaign mail and phone calls. In other states, which are considered safe for either the Democratic or Republican candidate, the presidential campaign is often so low key that it's almost invisible.

> *It's the independents who can make the difference in a candidate's election.*

... And Swing Voters ...

Just as there are swing states, there are also swing voters—individuals who don't necessarily vote along party lines or whose votes are still up for grabs. With the number of independent voters a sizeable 10 to 12 percent of the American electorate in recent years, presidential campaigns have focused on attracting the support of this all-important group.

After all, loyal partisans on both sides are very likely to support their party's candidate no matter what, and it's the independents who can make the difference in a candidate's election (see chapter 3 for more on independent voting).

But it's not just independent voters whom the candidates are trying to "swing." It's also voters who are registered with the other party but who have shown they don't have a problem crossing party lines.

In the 1980s, for example, much of President Ronald Reagan's success at the ballot box was attributed to "Reagan Democrats." These were Democratic voters—many of them rank-and-file union members—who had become disillusioned with their party and were willing to support the Republican presidential candidate.

... Without Ignoring Your Base

The importance of swing states and swing voters doesn't mean the candidates can ignore their most loyal supporters; in fact, they do so at their peril. For the candidates, the parties, and independent organizations, a major focus as Election Day approaches is to organize comprehensive get-out-the-vote (GOTV) campaigns that bring loyal voters to the polls.

An important target of Democratic GOTV campaigns is minority voters, especially African Americans and Latinos. For Republicans, Christian conservatives provide a reliable base of support—and a good target for GOTV efforts.

Campaign Tactics, Part I: The Candidates in Control

Not long ago, the political parties played a major role in orchestrating their nominees' campaigns. But with the rise of the primary system and television in the late twentieth century, party regulars

NEGATIVE OR NOT? THAT IS THE QUESTION

One of the major strategy decisions facing a presidential candidate during the general election is whether to "go negative" against an opponent. Going negative doesn't mean critiquing another candidate's ideas and policy prescriptions; that kind of debate can and should be an integral part of the campaign process. Rather, going negative means going after candidates themselves—attacking their competence and character.

Under some circumstances, such an approach might be legitimate. But beware. More often than not, negative campaigning is a deliberate effort to steer the debate away from the important issues facing the country.

The growth of 527 committees (see page 41) and other groups that are partisan but officially independent has opened new ways to go negative without making one's own favored candidate or party seem mean-spirited. In 2004, for example, the 527 committee Swift Boat Veterans for Truth attacked the Vietnam war record of Democrat John Kerry. Since the group was independent, the Bush campaign could not be blamed for the negative tone of the ads or their questionable content.

lost control of the process, and candidates became increasingly independent. Today's presidential contenders are able to talk directly to the voters through the mass media, instead of having to rely exclusively on their parties to get out the message.

Ever since Dwight Eisenhower ran for the White House in 1952, presidential candidates have created national organizations that are independent of the parties to run their campaigns. The Federal Election Campaign Act, which establishes the rules for presidential campaign financing, requires candidates to create national organizations to handle campaign contributions and expenditures. As campaigns have grown more complex, these campaign organizations have become more professional, relying on political consultants, media experts, and pollsters to plot strategy and provide information and advice. The campaign generally has a close relationship with the national party, with the presidential campaign playing the dominant role.

Sometimes, a candidate's campaign organization itself makes news—for example, when there is dissension within the ranks, or when someone new is brought in to manage key aspects of the campaign. The media generally jump on such stories as an indication that the campaign is in trouble. And critics inevitably suggest that if the candidate can't manage a presidential campaign, how can he or she manage the country?

A finely tuned and cohesive campaign organization, by contrast, can make the difference in steering a candidate to victory.

A finely tuned and cohesive campaign organization, by contrast, can make the difference in steering a candidate to victory. Bill Clinton's 1992 campaign—with its relentless focus on the state of the U.S. economy—is regularly cited as a model of how candidates and their organizations need to stay disciplined and "on message" if they are to win.

The candidates' top advisers can also play an essential role in keeping a campaign on track. James Carville, the "ragin' Cajun," played that role for Bill Clinton. And many observers believe that senior campaign strategist Karl Rove was essential to George W.

Bush's victories in 2000 and 2004. Rove was a voracious acquirer of information, which he then used to plan both the grand strategy and the details of the two Bush campaigns.

Campaign Tactics, Part II: A Little Help from My Friends

The candidates and their organizations aren't alone in waging their campaigns, however. The political parties still play very important roles in promoting their nominees. After the campaign organizations themselves, the parties are the most important players. No other organizations have the organizational bases, or can spend as much money, as the parties.

Expect 2008 to be far and away the most expensive presidential election in U.S. history.

In fact, the parties' ever-growing use of special-interest contributions to pay for political advertisements and other election-related activities was one of the main reasons for the passage of the campaign reform act of 2002 (BCRA). Under this law, the party national committees are no longer able to receive "soft money" (that is, contributions not limited by federal law). But thanks to vigorous fund-raising efforts, both the Democratic and Republican parties were able to raise as much money in "hard money" (federally regulated contributions) from many small donors as they had previously been able to raise in large, unregulated contributions. So the national parties are still very important players in the presidential campaign. State and local parties also work for presidential candidates, along with their work on a slew of other campaigns—congressional, state, and local.

Many observers feel that the parties today are not as dominant a force as in the past, but merely extensions of the candidates' campaign organizations—raising funds, producing and buying advertising, recruiting volunteers, and organizing get-out-the-vote efforts for the candidates.

Both the parties and the candidates also receive help in the form of advertising, volunteers, and on-the-ground support from major interest groups such as business, labor, and single-issue groups, like the National Rifle Association (see chapter 3).

MONEY TALKS

Campaign finance rules have a profound effect on the candidates' strategy for the general election. In fact, one of the first major decisions a campaign organization has to make is whether to accept federal funds and the accompanying limits on campaign spending, or whether to operate entirely with private financing.

As discussed in chapter 5, candidates are under increasing financial pressure to forgo public funding and campaign strictly on the money they and their allies are able to raise privately. In large part, that's because the presidential funding system has not kept up with the front-loaded campaign schedule and the higher levels of funds needed to run a viable campaign.

In 2004, both Republican George W. Bush and Democrat John Kerry skipped federal funding for the primary elections, but accepted public funding for the general election. As this book was written in 2007, it was uncertain whether the major candidates would accept federal funding at all in 2008. If the candidates forgo public funding in both the primaries and the general election, that means they won't have to abide by spending limits either. In that case, expect 2008 to be far and away the most expensive presidential election in U.S. history. Parties and interest groups also spend millions on the presidential campaign (see chapter 5).

Whether or not a candidate is operating under the federal limits on spending, an important strategic decision is how much of the budget to spend on television and other advertising and when and where to target it. Because advertising is so expensive, the campaigns have to be careful about how they're spending their ad dollars. The key is to be "on the air" at critical times during the campaign—particularly in the final weeks before the voting—and to target advertising on key states.

Campaign Tactics, Part III: Four Campaigns at Once

Today's presidential candidates essentially wage four campaigns at the same time. The first is the grassroots campaign. While the candidates themselves have little direct involvement in it, national campaign staff help to give it direction. It includes hundreds of local campaign headquarters and party organizations, from which volunteers and a few paid staff reach out into local communities. They register voters, make phone calls, send out mail, help friendly voters apply for absentee ballots, put up signs, do door-to-door canvassing, and get out the vote on Election Day. While each of these activities is small in scale, when multiplied by thousands, their combined impact can carry a state.

During the presidential elections of 2000 and 2004, both won by George W. Bush, the Republican Party showed itself especially adept at grassroots mobilization. Karl Rove, Bush's senior strategist in both campaigns, was widely acknowledged to be a master at getting out the vote for his candidate. For example, Rove directed the campaigns to buy commercial databases showing the consumer habits and lifestyles of voters. Through "data-mining" this information, the campaign could devise ways of appealing to those voters in the most effective ways. The Bush campaign also used person-to-person outreach effectively, asking evangelical Christians, for example, to talk about the election with fellow parishioners.

The second level of campaigning is "on the ground," and includes all of the candidate's appearances and speeches, as well as the appearances throughout the country of key supporters, from the candidate's spouse and children to the vice presidential nominee, Hollywood celebrities, and prominent party leaders. The on-the-ground campaign is tightly controlled by the candidate's campaign organization, with advance teams scoping out locations, rounding up enthusiastic, cheering crowds, and creating compelling visuals for television by placing the candidate before a dramatic backdrop and distributing truckloads of banners, signs, and American flags among the crowd.

The primary goal of this ground campaign is to attract media attention—more specifically, to get the candidate and surrogates on the local television news. Unless it is an enormous event, more people will see the event on the news than in person, and if the television coverage presents the candidate in a favorable light, then the campaign has done its job. The ground campaign does serve other functions as well: It helps energize the candidate's supporters, build the organization, and turn out voters on Election Day.

THE THIRD-PARTY EFFECT

While the Democratic and Republican Parties have dominated U.S. politics for 140 years, the American political system allows other parties and independent candidates to run for office as well. Several times in the last twenty-five years, third-party candidates have gained enough votes to make a difference in the outcome of the presidential race.

In 1992 and 1996, businessman Ross Perot ran as an angry centrist tired of political corruption in Washington. In 1992, he got an extraordinarily high 19 percent of the popular vote. Some believe that he took more votes away from Republican George H. W. Bush than from Democrat Bill Clinton and therefore helped Clinton to victory. In 1996, Perot received 8 percent of the vote.

Progressive advocate Ralph Nader in 2000 ran as the Green Party candidate, gaining just 2.7 percent of the vote. Since Nader was running on an anti-corporate, environmentalist platform, he almost certainly took more votes from Democrat Al Gore than from Republican George W. Bush. Angry Democrats accused Nader of being a "spoiler," saying he effectively helped the candidate who was worse from his own political perspective (Bush). But Nader and the Greens responded that Gore was too pro-business to merit their support.

The third campaign in which the candidates are engaged is an on-the-air battle of radio and television commercials. This advertising is the most expensive line item in the campaign budget—an estimated one-third of the more than $1.2 billion spent on the 2004 presidential campaign. Much of this money is spent through media consultants. The advertising gives the candidates massive nationwide exposure that they couldn't possibly achieve on the ground. It takes the campaign directly into voters' living rooms and allows the candidates to project a fine-tuned, poll-tested image.

The fourth and newest arena consists of the fast-evolving world of the Internet. This includes candidate Web sites and their presence on social networking sites like MySpace and Facebook, YouTube, Wikipedia, as well as campaign blogs (which also means monitoring the flow of messages in the blogosphere and responding quickly to them). One big challenge here is finding staffers who are both politically savvy and who understand the norms of Web communities well enough to win "friends" for their candidates and generally make their bosses look cool.

THE DEBATES: A VIEWER'S GUIDE

Some suggestions on what a savvy observer might look for in the fall debates between the major candidates.

- Identify the candidate's debate strategy. Does the candidate speak directly to the issues, provide specifics, and present new policies or information? Or is the candidate being more cautious, perhaps seeking to protect a lead in the opinion polls? Is the candidate spending more time attacking the opponent(s) than explaining his or her own views?
- Pay close attention when the candidates talk about how to solve problems. How detailed are their policy prescriptions, or are they trying to keep things vague?
- Think about what issues concern you most. Listen carefully to the candidates' answers on the issues you care most about. How do they compare with your own views on those issues? Does it sound like those issues are a priority for the candidates?
- Don't let appearances guide your reactions. A common criticism of debates is that they are driven by image and appearances. Try to listen for the substance of the speakers' answers.
- Don't watch a debate to determine a winner or loser. The news media often race to determine a victor in the debate, but this doesn't mean you have to, too. The key question is not who won or lost the debate, but which of the candidates you feel would make a better president.

The Candidates Face Off: The Presidential Debates

One place on the campaign trail where the candidates are guaranteed to get at least a few difficult questions is at the presidential debates. The debates, held in October, are the only time during the general election campaign when the major contenders appear together to discuss the issues in the election. As we've discussed, most candidates also participate in an earlier round of debates in which contenders from within one party are seeking their party's nomination.

Debates provide the candidates with an opportunity to present their views directly to a national audience, without having to pay for the time or filter their message through the media. For voters, debates provide a chance to judge the candidates side by side while they articulate their views and perhaps reveal something of their characters.

During recent presidential elections, debate formats have varied. They have included:

+ A press-conference format, where a panel of journalists asks the candidates questions
+ A debate with a single moderator who asks the candidates questions and who can ask follow-up questions if the original answers are deemed not satisfactory
+ Town-hall debates, in which the candidates face questions from voters in the audience

Many candidates prefer to keep the debates as tightly formatted as possible so they can make a polished and scripted presentation. Negotiations over the number and format of the debates have become a regular feature of the fall campaign season. But the pressure on the candidates to debate has become intense; not debating is really not an option, because candidates' opponents will be likely to score political points over their reluctance to face the voters.

Just as with other kinds of political activity, the percentage of Americans who watch the presidential debates has dropped in recent decades. More than half of U.S. households had their TVs tuned to the debates in both 1976 and 1980, reported Thomas

Patterson in *The Vanishing Voter.* This fell to 36 percent in 1988 and
to 29 percent in 1996 and 2000. Surprisingly, interest in the debates
spiked enormously in 2004, with about 67 percent of Americans
polled saying they watched at least part of the first Bush-Kerry
debate. One possible reason for the change: Polls indicated that the
Iraq conflict sparked interest in the presidential campaign and the
debates.

Even in years of low viewer interest, the debates get Americans
talking and thinking about the candidates. In 2000, the number
of Americans who recognized Bush's and Gore's positions on the issues increased by 25 percent during the debates.

*Interest in the
debates spiked
enormously in
2004, with about
67 percent of
Americans polled
saying they
watched at least
part of the first
Bush-Kerry debate.*

In some cases, debates can significantly improve or worsen how the public perceives a candidate. Whether the debates help or hurt a candidate may not simply be a matter of who "wins" the debate. For example, George W. Bush was perceived more favorably after the October 2000 debates, some observers say, because he performed better than expected against Al Gore. Doubts about whether Bush was intellectually up to the job were allayed when he held his own against the vice president, who was widely seen as having greater policy expertise. Just as important, Bush was portrayed as more likable than Gore in the media coverage surrounding the debates.

What About the Issues?

While a presidential campaign may seem like the ideal time
to have a prolonged discussion of the most serious issues facing
America, that seldom happens. Campaigns test all their messages
through polls and often wind up focusing on relatively small issues
that they believe will impress voters. Or they focus on the supposed
characters of the two candidates, explaining why their candidate is a
real American, a regular guy who cares about people like you, while
the other candidate is untrustworthy or elitist or a phony.

What are the important issues? A Gallup poll in April 2007 indicated that these were the issues that would be important to registered voters when they went to the polls in 2008. (Of course, those could change enormously by November 2008.)

War issues in Iraq	43 %
The economy	15 %
Healthcare/health insurance	10 %
Homeland security/military defense	7 %
Education	6 %
Illegal immigration	5 %

A number of other issues are important to the nation's, and even the world's, future, such as global warming, the aging U.S. population and the pressures that will bring on Social Security and healthcare, the American people's zero savings rate, and America's huge and persistent trade deficit and federal budget deficit.

Will those questions be discussed in the 2008 campaign? Chances are that will happen only if a campaign can see a way to package the issue with a simple appeal that works to its advantage.

This is your country and your life, so get into the driver's seat and help steer this country in the direction you think is best.

It's Your Choice!

The League of Women Voters urges all U.S. citizens and voters to take the election seriously. This is your country and your life, so get into the driver's seat and help steer this country in the direction you think is best.

Some basic things you can do:

1. Register to vote. See page 15 in chapter 1 on how to do that.
2. Find out about the candidates and their positions: read the papers, check the Web sites.
3. Decide what you're looking for in a candidate.
4. Evaluate the candidates' stands on the issues important to you.

5. Learn about the candidates' leadership abilities.
6. "Talk" about the candidates and issues with friends, relatives, coworkers, whether that means e-mailing, instant-messaging, blogging, or even having face-to-face conversations.
7. Make sure you have the correct ID required in your state (many states have been changing their laws on this) and that you know where to vote. Fifty percent of calls received on Election Day hotlines are from voters asking about their polling place. The League of Women Voters' site — www.VOTE411.org — provides this information.
8. Vote (and if it's hard to get to the polls on Election Day, remember that absentee ballots are generally easy to cast).

CHAPTER 10

Election Day

On the Tuesday in November that falls between November 2 and November 8, control of the presidential election finally passes into the hands of the American voter—where it belongs. After all the ceaseless campaigning by the candidates, all the news coverage, television and radio advertising, videos, blogging and expert punditry, and all the hard work by the candidate's supporters, it comes down to this: the voters' decision about which of the candidates they feel is most qualified to lead the nation.

Election Day is November 4, 2008.

As we've noted in earlier chapters, not everyone votes on Election Day (that's November 4 in 2008), so the term is becoming something of a misnomer. Hoping to boost voter turnout, states are increasingly allowing voters to vote as much as a month early, by mail or in person. In fact, in November 2004, about one in five American voters cast ballots before Election Day. That may help turnout, and it also means that campaigns now have to reach out to early voters in new ways—for example, keeping track of who has applied for absentee ballots.

A Work in Progress

Until the 2000 election, most people in America took for granted that our elections were conducted fairly and accurately. Stories about big-city political machines stuffing ballot boxes seemed to belong to the Dark Ages. But the people who ran the elections, and people who studied elections, always knew the system was imperfect. There were always voters who were supposed to be registered but somehow weren't on the rolls, or people who messed up their ballots so they couldn't be counted.

But in November 2000, the presidential election went undecided for thirty-six days after the official Election Day. For the most part, the long, confusing stalemate revolved around voting procedures in

Until the 2000 election, most people in America took for granted that our elections were conducted fairly and accurately.

Florida—ballots that were badly designed, votes that were hard to decipher, counting rules that changed from day to day. It was a mess. (See the box "The Amazing Florida Recount of 2000" below for more details.)

A positive result of the disastrous Florida election was that it focused the states' and Congress's attention on the need to fix the defects in our voting systems. Careful examination of Florida's problems revealed that some voting devices, especially computer punch-card systems, were error-prone. Overall error rates on voting machines commonly used in the United States were found to run anywhere from 0.5 percent to 4 percent—that's enough to change many election results! And these kinds of problems could be found in every state in the Union.

THE AMAZING FLORIDA RECOUNT OF 2000

As the presidential election came to a close on the night of Nov. 7, 2000, Americans learned, much to their surprise, that no one knew who the winner was. The race between Democrat Al Gore and Republican George Bush was so close that the outcome depended on which candidate took Florida—and Florida was too close to call.

For the next thirty-six days, America went on an amazing and confusing political journey as the two candidates and their supporters slugged it out. Americans learned that the process of counting votes is not simple—it can depend on who's counting and what the rules are.

After the first Florida recount, Bush was ahead by just 327 votes, out of nearly 6 million cast. But in the United States as a whole, Gore led the popular vote, which encouraged the Democrats to keep fighting.

As the recount dragged on for five weeks, an anxious public watched as:

- Badly designed ballots in Palm Beach County led to thousands of disqualified votes.
- Punch-card voting in three big counties produced ballots that were hard to interpret. Americans learned that a "hanging chad" meant a bit of paper that was partly but not entirely punched out of a voter's card.
- African Americans' votes were disqualified more often than white people's votes.
- Recounts stopped and started as the Gore and Bush teams argued in state courts about the legality and procedures of recounts.

Throughout the long recount, Bush's margin remained small, but Gore never pulled into the lead. Finally, the Bush team appealed to the U.S. Supreme Court, which ordered all Florida recounts stopped. That meant that Bush won.

Bush now had 271 votes in the Electoral College, one more than the 270 needed. He also became one of the few people in U.S. history to win the presidency without winning the popular vote.

The drawn-out, confusing Florida recount clearly strengthened the case for reform of the U.S. voting system. One result was the Help America Vote Act of 2002 (see page 154), which gets rid of punch-card ballots, sets nationwide standards for the conduct of elections, and offers states financial help in improving their voting systems.

The Help America Vote Act

Spurred by the enormity of the disarray, Congress in October 2002 passed the Help America Vote Act (HAVA), which creates new national standards for how citizens register and vote. A very important feature of the new law is that, for the first time, the federal government is helping states and localities with funds to improve election procedures.

Another essential change is that the law gives increased authority over elections to the state governments, with the goal of instituting uniform and nondiscriminatory practices within each state. Among the highlights of the law:

+ States were required to establish centralized, computerized databases of voter registrations. These can be linked to other databases, such as those for driver's licenses. The goal is for each state to have one clean, up-to-date voter list, eliminating duplications.
+ Voters who show up at a polling place but are not on the voters' rolls are now given a provisional ballot and permitted to vote—instead of being turned away. If it is found that they really are eligible to vote, their votes are counted (as most were in 2004).
+ First-time voters who register by mail must verify their identity, either when they register or when they vote, by providing their driver's license number or the last four digits of their Social Security number. If they can't provide either, the state assigns them a unique identifier.
+ Funds have been made available to replace punch-card voting systems and old-fashioned lever voting machines. Federal funds can also be used for other purposes, such as training poll workers.
+ Voters must be allowed to check their ballots and correct errors before they leave the polling place.

Implementation of the HAVA rules began in 2004; they are supposed to be in effect in all polling stations in 2008.

HAVA initially authorized about $3.9 billion in funding to help the states meet the law's mandates. In its first three years of operation, about $3 billion of that was distributed, but by 2006 funds were in short supply, leading states to wonder if they would be able to complete implementation.

One important result of HAVA has been a marked shift in the type of voting machines Americans used. Punch-card machines are almost entirely gone, and lever machines are being phased out. But touch-screen machines, which are acceptable under HAVA, have been strongly criticized because they normally leave no "paper trail." That is, because they are entirely computerized, they usually provide no independently verifiable way to do a recount.

A College Education: How Does the Electoral College Work?

You'd think that the election of the president and vice president would be a relatively simple matter—whoever gets the most votes wins. But it's a lot more complicated than that. Instead of providing that the president and vice president should be chosen directly by voters, the U.S. Constitution created an institution called the Electoral College that actually casts the deciding vote. The Electoral College was one of the many ways in which our founders tried to keep "popular passions" from steering the national government in the wrong direction.

In the beginning, the Electoral College had considerable power in making an independent choice among the candidates for president and vice president. But today, the sole function of the Electoral College is to confirm the decision made by American voters at the ballot box. In other words, despite the existence of the Electoral College, voters still are in the driver's seat in determining who will serve as president. So don't think your vote doesn't count.

Today, the sole function of the Electoral College is to confirm the decision made by American voters at the ballot box.

Under the Constitution, each state is authorized to choose electors for president and vice president; the number of electors per state is equal to the combined number of U.S. senators and representatives from that state. The Electoral College thus includes 535 electors from the states—that's one elector for every member of Congress—plus three electors from the District of Columbia, for a grand total of 538.

When voters choose a presidential ticket including the presidential and vice presidential candidate, they are actually voting for electors pledged to this ticket. In all but two states, the ticket that wins a plurality of the votes—in other words, more votes than any other candidate—wins all of that state's electors. (In Maine and Nebraska, the candidate who wins the state's popular vote gets two electoral votes; the others are awarded according to who wins each congressional district.) This winner-take-all system is what drives candidates to focus so intently in their campaigning on swing states with large populations and, consequently, large numbers of electors (see chapter 9 for more on campaign strategy).

To be elected to the presidency, a candidate must receive an absolute majority (270) of the electoral votes. The vice president is elected by the same indirect, state-by-state method, but the electors vote separately for the two offices.

Two candidates in the nineteenth century, as well as George W. Bush in 2000, were elected president without winning the popular vote.

If no presidential candidate receives a majority, the House of Representatives picks the winner from the top three vote getters, with each state's delegation in the House casting only one vote, regardless of its size. (This has happened twice in U.S. history—in 1800 and 1824.) If no vice presidential candidate receives a majority, the Senate picks the winner from the top two vote getters.

Do We Really Need the Electoral College? Proposals for Change

Over the years, Congress has debated a number of changes in the Electoral College system. Most of these would require enactment of a constitutional amendment, although individual states can change their own laws governing how they choose electors. Some people suggest we keep the Electoral College but eliminate the

THE ELECTORAL COLLEGE: PRO AND CON

PRO

It Ain't Broke, So Don't Fix It
For the past one hundred years, the Electoral College has functioned without a problem and without much complaint from the public in every presidential election—through two world wars, a major economic depression, and several periods of civil unrest.

It Fosters the Two-Party System
The winner-take-all system (in all but two states) generally means that third-party and independent candidates get few electoral votes. As a result, the Electoral College inhibits the rise of splinter parties that can contribute to political instability and deadlock. (Note: Some people use this argument against the Electoral College, saying its bias against third-party and independent candidates locks them out of the process and inhibits debate.)

It Gives Added Power to Minority Groups
Because of the winner-take-all system, a relatively small number of voters in a state can make the difference in determining which candidate gets that state's electoral votes. This gives well-organized minority groups a chance to have a profound influence on the election by getting their voters to the polls.

It Promotes a Federal System of Government
The Electoral College was designed to reflect each state's choice for the presidency and vice presidency. To abolish it in favor of a nationwide popular election of the president would strike at the very heart of our federal system of government, which reserves important political powers to the states.

CON

It Ignores the Popular Vote
The Electoral College doesn't base its decision on the popular vote across the country, but on which candidates won which states. As a result, there's a chance that someone could be

elected president without receiving more popular votes than any other candidates. Two candidates in the nineteenth century, as well as George W. Bush in 2000, were elected president without winning the popular vote.

It Discourages Voter Turnout
The Electoral College system makes many people feel that their vote doesn't make a difference. Voters might be inclined to skip voting, for example, if it's clear from the news and the polls that Candidate X is bound to win their state.

It Violates the One-Person One-Vote Ideal
Each state has a minimum of three electors, regardless of its population. This gives residents of the smallest states, which based on their population might otherwise be entitled to just one or two electors, more influence than residents of larger states.

It Doesn't Require Electors to Vote the Way They Pledged To
It rarely happens, but there's nothing preventing electors from defecting from the candidate to whom they are pledged. In 2000, an elector from the District of Columbia abstained from voting to protest what she called D.C.'s "colonial status." Faithless electors could conceivably alter who wins the election, though none ever has.

winner-take-all rule so that a state's electors would better reflect the preferences of all the voters in the state. Under this scenario, a state's electors would either be chosen on a congressional district basis or simply assigned to the candidates based on the percentage of the popular vote each received in the state. For example, if Candidate X received 20 percent of the popular vote in Arizona, that person would be awarded 20 percent of the state's electoral votes.

These changes might bring the electoral vote more in line with the popular vote, but voters still would be electing the president indirectly. The Electoral College, in other words, would still exist.

Another reform proposal would have states award their electoral votes to the candidate who wins the most popular votes nationwide. This concept, if implemented, would encourage candidates to pay attention to voters all across the United States, not just in key swing states. The innovative idea got a boost in 2007, when the Maryland legislature made it state law. But the Maryland law only kicks in if states that together hold 270 electoral votes (enough to win a presidential election) agree to do the same.

The Electoral College gives the smaller-population states a bigger say in the election than they would have under direct election of the president.

In the 1970s, Congress debated a proposal to eliminate the Electoral College. But that was defeated in the Senate, and since then proposals to reform or abolish the Electoral College have gained little traction on Capitol Hill. A major reason we still have the Electoral College is that it gives the smaller-population states a bigger say in the election than they would have under direct election of the president. It's not likely that these states will voluntarily give up their extra influence over the choice of president.

Tabulating the Outcome: The Results Are In!

Before the advent of television, electronic voting machines, and computerized balloting, it could take days or even weeks for the nation to know whom it had elected president. But starting in the 1950s, and accelerating in later decades, this process changed. The national networks began coverage of election returns while the polls were still open and continued until the results were known, which generally didn't take very long. Thanks to computerized tabulation of ballots and a technique known as exit polling, the winner was often announced just hours after the polls had closed. Eager to report on the election results as soon as possible, the news media came up with a method for projecting a winner while the returns still were coming in, even if only 5 percent or fewer of the precincts had reported their results. The media accomplished this by assigning people to interview voters on their way out of the polling place to find out how they voted.

These exit interviews allow the television networks and major newspapers to track the voting in key precincts whose returns usually

parallel the complete returns for their states. Based on the exit interviews, a newscaster often was able to tell viewers which candidate had
carried a certain state just minutes after the polls in the state had closed.
As the night went on, the television networks competed to identify
which candidate had won enough states to amass the 270 electoral
votes needed to win the election. Exit polls also allowed the media
to gauge how various categories of voters—say, men and women—
felt about the candidates and the issues. The voters' answers gave the
newscasters something to talk about while they were waiting for the
next states' polls to close. Beyond this, exit polls give political scientists
and analysts an excellent opportunity to find out why people vote the
way they do. It's the best measure, because voters answer questions
right after the event, when their recollections are likely to be accurate.

Early Projections: Jumping the Gun

Early projections of election results became a controversial public
issue. Critics said that by predicting the outcome while Americans
were still voting, the media were in effect discouraging some people
from voting. This concern reached a peak in 1980, when Ronald
Reagan's victory over Jimmy Carter was announced by all the networks before the polls had even closed in the West. It is quite possible that some West Coast residents heard the news and didn't
bother to go to the polls—after all, the election was already decided.
An academic study published in 1983 declared, "Hearing news of
the projected outcome decreased the likelihood of voting among
those who had not already voted." This may have changed the outcome in congressional, state, and local elections.

As a result of these concerns, the major broadcast and cable networks decided to wait until a state's polls have closed before reporting election results for that state. But they were still able to project
a winner of the presidential election before the polls had closed in
all states across the country. In addition, the media emphatically
point out that their First Amendment right to freedom of the press
would be violated by any restrictions on their announcing election
winners. Given the competitive nature of the media, it is highly
unlikely that the winner would not be announced by at least one
news source, and then the others would immediately follow.

ELECTORAL VOTES BY STATE

This chart shows how many electoral votes each state will have in the 2008 election. Every ten years after the U.S. Census, the number of electors is adjusted to take into account population changes. The current allocation reflects the 2000 Census. Because of long-term population trends, a number of Southern and Western states gained congressional seats, and therefore Electoral College votes, after the 2000 Census. Several states in the Northeast and Midwest lost congressional seats.

TOTAL: 538 NEEDED TO WIN: 270

Electoral Votes in 2008

State	Votes	State	Votes
California	55	Connecticut	7
Texas	34	Iowa	7
New York	31	Oklahoma	7
Florida	27	Oregon	7
Illinois	21	Arkansas	6
Pennsylvania	21	Kansas	6
Ohio	20	Mississippi	6
Michigan	17	Nebraska	5
Georgia	15	Nevada	5
New Jersey	15	New Mexico	5
North Carolina	15	Utah	5
Virginia	13	West Virginia	5
Massachusetts	12	Hawaii	4
Indiana	11	Idaho	4
Missouri	11	Maine	4
Tennessee	11	New Hampshire	4
Washington	11	Rhode Island	4
Arizona	10	Alaska	3
Maryland	10	Delaware	3
Minnesota	10	District of Columbia	3
Wisconsin	10	Montana	3
Alabama	9	North Dakota	3
Colorado	9	South Dakota	3
Louisiana	9	Vermont	3
Kentucky	8	Wyoming	3
South Carolina	8		

In Canada—a country which, like the United States, stretches across several time zones—federal law prohibits the media from reporting early election results in areas where the polls are still open. But in the Internet age, such a prohibition is no longer very effective.

Until the 2000 election, it seemed as if the American people would keep finding out election results earlier with each election. But a surprising thing happened in 2000: The largest and most sophisticated polling and prediction system—the Voter News Service—made serious errors, which was an embarrassing setback for the major news media that had been counting on its results. On election night in the crucial swing state of Florida, the polling service first called the state for Gore, then called it for Bush, and finally admitted it just didn't know. (See box, "The Amazing Florida Recount," page 152.)

The Voter News Service had been put together in the late 1980s by a partnership of television networks, the Associated Press, and other major news media. Its goal was to save the news organizations money by pooling resources into one big, computerized system. Two years later, in the elections of November 2002, the Voter News Service—after throwing out the old system and trying something completely new—did even worse than it had in 2000. Soon after, the service was shut down by its owners.

But this doesn't mean we've seen the end of exit polling and early projections. The attraction of getting early results is just too great, especially for television.

In fact, in January 2003, shortly after the Voter News Service folded, the three major TV networks and FOX, CNN, and the Associated Press formed a new consortium called the National Election Pool to do exit polling and give the media early election-night results. The new organization performed reasonably well in 2004 and 2006, though in 2004, early exit poll results were leaked, which gave a mistakenly positive picture of how well John Kerry was doing in the presidential election.

Making It Official

Normally, by the morning after the election, the final results are in, and the entire country knows who the next president and vice

THE OHIO CONTROVERSY OF 2004

The nation faced another close election in 2004, between President George W. Bush and Democratic challenger Senator John Kerry. This time the key swing state that might decide the overall result was Ohio.

But on Election Day, a number of odd events occurred in the Ohio voting. For one thing, as noted earlier, exit polls showed Kerry in the lead, while the official count showed Bush carrying the state by 118,000 votes. Some Ohio precincts had terribly long lines—the longest wait in the nation was eleven hours in one college town. In Franklin County, Ohio, one precinct for a while reported nearly 4,000 votes for Bush, although the precinct had fewer than 800 voters.

All this led many Democratic activists and many progressives in the blogosphere to claim that massive vote fraud had been perpetrated in Ohio. Some claimed that the Republicans were "stealing the election," as they had in Florida in 2000. When the smoke cleared, most of the vote count problems were cleared up and explained.

But as in Florida, the Election Day confusion revealed a voting system with many defects. The League of Women Voters of Ohio filed a lawsuit against the state of Ohio, not challenging the 2004 results, but demanding a fair, accurate, and voter-friendly election system in the future.

In Congress on January 5, 2005, when it came time to certify the results of the presidential election, thirty-one members of the House and one senator challenged Ohio's Electoral College vote. It was the first such challenge since 1877. After a four-hour debate, however, Congress awarded Ohio's 20 electoral votes to Bush, who thus had 286 electoral votes to Kerry's 252. The president was re-elected.

president will be. But whether we have a normal election or a contested one, the outcome still has to be made official. In December, the members of the Electoral College travel to their state capitals to cast their official electoral votes, sign some necessary documents, and pose for pictures, before returning home. When Congress convenes in January, senators and representatives gather for a joint congressional session, and the official results are announced from all the states.

At noon on January 20, 2009, the term of George W. Bush ends and that of the incoming president begins.

At noon on the 20th of January following a presidential election, the term of the preceding president ends and that of the incoming president begins. At a formal inauguration ceremony, the chief justice of the U.S. Supreme Court swears in the president and the vice president before members of Congress, government dignitaries, representatives of foreign governments, and important well-wishers, as well as a national television audience.

After an inaugural address and parade, the new president is on the job. The American people have made their choice and are looking to the new president to prove them right.

OTHER WAYS OF VOTING?

Some observers believe that the American political system, as currently constituted, gives the American people too little choice. Generally, they say, voters get to choose between the two major parties, and any other options tend to be squeezed out. That's because when we cast a single vote for a single candidate, a vote for anyone other than the two top candidates can seem like a wasted vote.

Is it possible to open up the U.S. political system, to make it more welcoming to other choices and parties?

One possibility, used in Ireland and Australia, is "instant runoff voting." In this system, you don't just vote for your favorite candidate—you mark a series of preferences: choice number one, then two, then three, as many as you choose. When ballots are counted, if your number one choice has the lowest vote total, then that candidate's votes are redistributed to your number two choice.

So, for example, if your number one choice is Nader and your number two choice is Gore, when Nader is eliminated from the competition, your vote is transferred and becomes a Gore vote. This method of voting allows third (and fourth, and fifth) parties to run candidates for office without worrying about becoming "spoilers."

Another way to open up the system is called "fusion" voting, which is practiced in New York State. It permits a party to endorse another party's candidates and have that candidate run on its own party line.

So, for example, if the Right to Life Party decides that the Republican candidate is strong on its issues, it can make the Republican candidate its nominee, too. Then people can vote for this candidate either on the Republican ticket or on the Right to Life ticket. All votes for the candidate, under any party designation, are counted. Fusion voting, like instant runoff voting, helps create a political space in which third parties can thrive.

Bibliography and Videography

Armstrong, Jerome, and Markos Moulitsas Zúniga. *Crashing the Gate: Netroots, Grassroots, and the Rise of People-Powered Politics.* White River Junction, Vt.: Chelsea Green, 2006.

Campbell, James E. *American Campaign: U.S. Presidential Campaigns and the National Vote.* College Station, Tex.: Texas A&M University Press, 2000.

Corrado, Anthony, et al. *The New Campaign Finance Sourcebook.* Washington, D.C.: Brookings Institution, 2005. Also available at www.brook.edu/gs/cf/newsourcebk.htm.

Halperin, Mark, and John F. Harris. *The Way to Win: Taking the White House in 2008.* New York: Random House, 2006.

Malbin, Michael J., editor. *Life After Reform: When the Bipartisan Campaign Reform Act Meets Politics.* Lanham, Md.: Rowman & Littlefield, 2006.

Matalin, Mary, and James Carville, with Peter Knobler. *All's Fair: Love, War and Running for President.* New York: Random House, 1994.

Patterson, Thomas E. *The Vanishing Voter: Public Involvement in an Age of Uncertainty.* New York: Alfred A. Knopf, 2002.

Plano, Jack, and Milton Greenberg. *The American Political Dictionary,* 11th ed. Beverly, Mass.: Wadsworth Publishing, 2001.

Sabato, Larry J., editor. *Divided States of America: The Slash and Burn Politics of the 2004 Presidential Election.* Boston: Longman Publishing, 2005.

Thomas, Evan, and the staff of Newsweek. *Election 2004: How Bush Won and What You Can Expect in the Future.* New York: Public Affairs, 2004.

Toobin, Jeffrey. *Too Close to Call: The Thirty-Six Day Battle to Decide the 2000 Election.* New York: Random House, 2001.

Washington Post (Ellen Nakashima, et al.). *Deadlock: The Inside Story of America's Closest Election.* New York: Public Affairs, 2001.

Annotated Videography

The War Room. Behind-the-scenes documentary of Bill Clinton's beleaguered but successful presidential campaign of 1992. Considerable insight and humor. Starring James Carville and George Stephanopoulos. Skillfully directed by D. A. Pennebaker and Chris Hegedus.

Journeys with George. This documentary follows the 2000 campaign of George W. Bush and how he engaged with (and, for the most part, won over) the press contingent that covered him. Co-directed and narrated by Alexandra Pelosi, daughter of Representative (and now Speaker of the House) Nancy Pelosi, D-Calif.

Tanner '88. A five-hour mini-series written by Garry Trudeau (Doonesbury) and directed by Robert Altman (MASH). An account of a fictional presidential candidate, Jack Tanner, filmed against the backdrop of real politicians playing themselves during the 1988 primaries and convention. Thought-provoking and funny.

INDEX